Alastair Reid

Whereabouts

Notes on Being a Foreigner

T0131408

White Pine Press

A hardcover edition of this book was published in 1987 by
North Point Press and is reprinted here by arrangement
with them.

ISBN: 978-1-945-68022-9

"Digging Up Scotland," "Hauntings," "Basilisks' Eggs,"
and "Notes from a Spanish Village" first appeared in *The
New Yorker*, "In Memoriam, Amada" in the *New York Review
of Books*, and "Other People's Houses" in *House & Garden*. "Notes on Being a Foreigner" is reprinted from *Passwords: Places: Poems, Preoccupations* (Atlantic/Little, Brown,
1963). The poems, "Speaking a Foreign Language," "Scotland," "The Academy," "My Father Dying" and "The
Manse," are reprinted from *Weathering: Poems and Translations* (Dutton, 1978).

Design by Watershed Design

Cover artwork by Elaine LaMattina

Publication of this book was made possible, in part, by
grants from the National Endowment for the Arts and the
New York State Council on the Arts.

WHITE PINE PRESS
P.O. Box 236
Buffalo, N.Y. 14201

76 Center Street
Fredonia, N.Y. 14063

for John Alexander Coleman
and Thomas Colchie

se todos fossem no mundo iguais a vocês

Contents

Whereabouts

Foreword

I had never thought of being other than a poet, of writing other than poetry, until I came to earth by pure chance in Spain during the fifties. I had first left Scotland during the war, the latter part of which I spent at sea, in the East; and then I had gone to the United States. These shiftings had been liberating, eye-widening, in quite different ways; but stumbling on Spain made more of a difference, for it meant that I had to enter another language, which amounts to starting a new life, naming the world again from the beginning. I felt more than illiterate, in that I had to learn again not just to read and write but also to speak. Something of that experience found its way into my poems; but beyond that, the oddness of being a foreigner sharpened my senses, and the Spanish present tugged insistently at my sleeve. I began writing prose chronicles from that paradoxical country for the *New Yorker*, and went on to write on a variety of matters for that magazine, from gypsies to cricket, thanks always to William Shawn, who tacitly encouraged me to follow my own nose.

In Spain, again by chance, I met Robert Graves, and for a time I spent part of each year in his village and in his company. I learned much from him by osmosis: when we worked together, translating Suetonius, I would pore over his scribbled corrections to my English versions, amazed at how much better he made them, and never forgetting how. Graves took both pride and pleasure in his craft: a writer, he stoutly maintained, should be able to put anything at all into words, to give it the form and language it asked for. To my ear, he wrote wonderful prose, spare and sinewy, always unmistakably his despite its great variety. He was fond of declaring that he "bred show dogs in order to be able to afford a cat," the dogs being prose, the cat poetry; but I did not subscribe to the distinction—except economically. Poetry and prose were to me two quite different modes of saying, but I always gave thanks for having written poetry first, hence bringing to prose the same charged attention, and phrasing by ear, as poets do. Poetry makes use of all the juices in language, while prose offers the possibilities of understatement. I love the long movement of prose, just as I love the miraculous compression of poetry. I prefer to think of the two modes as variations on the same impulse: to put-well-into-words.

Looking over the pieces collected here, I realize retrospectively how much my shifting state became the vantage point for my writings. The first piece, "Notes on Being a Foreigner," I wrote in Geneva in 1963, to pin down positively the feeling of being a foreigner, a condition that became second nature to me. Wherever I found myself, the ghosts of other places, other lives, hovered close: Scotland, where I had grown up and become aware; New York, where I spent vivid years, and where I felt warm; Spain, which I learned by heart; and, ultimately, the countries of Latin America. In Spain, I first read the Latin American writers, and I felt the same old-world curiosity about the New World that I had felt in Scotland about the United States. I made a pilgrimage round Latin America in 1964, and two friendships that began then—with Pablo Neruda and with Jorge Luis Borges—were to loom very large in my later life.

The two pieces, "Digging Up Scotland" and "Hauntings," represent my coming to terms with my flinty beginnings; but while I am still haunted by some Scottish landscapes and weathers, I never feel at home in the wariness of its human climate. On Saturday evenings, however, wherever I am, I try to tune in to the Scottish football results, and certain Scottish cadences go on sounding in my inner ear.

In Spain, I began to translate, mostly from curiosity, to see if

4

certain works could have an extended existence in English. Translating became something of an addiction, for, until I stopped translating recently, I usually had some translation in progress. I would translate for an hour or two every morning, as a kind of limbering up for writing. There is nothing more mysterious than shifting between languages, and I have always felt grateful to Octavio Paz for his observation: "... in writing an original poem we are translating the world, transmuting it. Everything we do is translation, and all translations are in a way creations ... the poet is ... the universal translator." I feel exactly that about writing, prose or poetry: it is all a matter of translating wordless perceptions into language, into words that will properly contain them. There is no clear point of arrival, no definitive version. There is only the endless business of looking for the right words and, sometimes, being lucky enough to find them.

Samaná, Dominican Republic
January 1986

Notes on
Being a Foreigner

I come suddenly into a foreign city, just as the lamps take light along the water, with some notes in my head. Arriving—the mood and excitement, at least, are always the same. I try out the language with the taxi driver, to see if it is still there; and later, I walk to a restaurant that is lurking round a corner in my memory. Nothing, of course, has changed; but cities flow on, like water, and, like water, they close behind any departure. We come back to confirm them, even though they do not particularly care. Or perhaps we come back to confirm ourselves?

•

By the time I have finished dinner, I find I have to make an effort to remember the place I left—how it felt, at least. Matches and toothpaste are the only continuities; once they are used up, the previous existence from which they came has withered and died. I walk along the snowy quais in the lamplit dark, breathing a tangle of strangeness and familiarity. Places are a little like old clothes. Wearing them brings nostalgia snowing down. There is both shock and recognition.

•

How easy it is to fall at once into the habits of a place, most noticeably the eating habits—to dine very late in Spain, to eat heartily in England, to change the whole conception of breakfast, to order certain kinds of drink instinctively. Another country is a new self, I am tempted to say—until I notice all the signs of the old self showing through.

•

Later, I telephone two or three friends, and am instantly drawn into a web of appointments, talk, question-and-answer, the nowheres of friendship, which supersede language, time, place. And somewhere, one of my friends is saying to someone I do not know yet: "So-and-so is coming for a drink. He is a foreigner."

•

Natives feel oddly toward foreigners. They may be hostile, aggressive, overfriendly, distant, or possessive; but at least they have the (to them) advantage of being in possession, so that between foreigners and themselves there is a moat with a drawbridge to which they keep the keys. Typical native gambits: "Why, we almost consider you one of us!" Or "What do you think of *our* (railways, king, public lavatories)?" Or "Are you familiar with our expression . . . ?" They have the assurance of Being In Possession.

•

And the foreigner? It depends on whether he is a foreigner by Necessity, Accident, or Choice. One thing, however, is sure: unless he regards being a foreigner as a positive state, he is doomed. If he has already chosen not to belong, then all the native gambits are bound to fail. But if he aspires to being a native, then he is forever at the mercy of the natives, down to the last inflection of the voice.

•

An expatriate shifts uncomfortably, because he still retains, at the back of his mind, the awareness that he has a true country, more real to him than any other he happens to have selected. Thus, he

7

is only at ease with other expatriates. They justify one another, as they wait about in the sun for the arrival of mail or money. Eventually, they are driven to talk of plumbing, the ultimate sign of the superiority of their own civilization. Whatever they do or write or say has its ultimate meaning for them Back Home. "Yes, but you have to make it in Boston," I once heard from a fanatical expatriate. What's more, he said it in Spanish.

•

Exiles, as opposed to expatriates, either wither away, or else flourish from being transplanted, depending on whether they keep alive any hope of returning to what they left, or abandon it completely as forever inaccessible. The hope of returning to the past, even at its faintest, makes for a vague unease, a dissatisfaction with the present. The Spanish exiles I knew were, for the most part, unhappy; Spain, after all, continued to exist, as they were always wistfully aware. The émigrés who left Russia after the Revolution took up, from necessity, another, healthier life, without thinking, and assumed new languages. America has been the most fruitful soil for exiles of all nationalities. America has no time for foreigners as such, being too preoccupied with its own tumultuous present, and being aggressively monoglot. If you are there, you are expected to contribute; you cannot just hang about, as you can in the more wistful cities of Europe. In America, you can join, or leave.

•

Tourists are to foreigners as occasional tipplers are to alcoholics—they take strangeness and alienation in small, exciting doses, and besides, they are well fortified against loneliness. Moreover, the places they visit expect and welcome them, put themselves out for their diversion. Boredom is the only hazard—it takes a healthy curiosity to keep tourists from rushing home in tears, from sighing with relief at the reappearance of familiarity. The principal difference between tourists and foreigners is that tourists have a home to go to, and a date of departure. I wonder how many of them would confess to have found the pinnacle of pleasure from a trip in the moment of returning home?

•

How appropriate tourists are, in certain places, at certain seasons! They set off spas, harbors, and watering places as pigeons set off cathedrals; they exude an appetite for pleasure and diversion. And often, they bring the best out of the places they visit; women who know they are going to be seen take more trouble with their appearance. The only thing that besets them is that they have to invent reasons for visiting the places they visit, or else suffer from their own pointlessness. And the sun, they discover, is not quite sufficient reason for being anywhere.

•

A foreigner has a curious perspective on the country he alights in. His foreignness more or less absolves him from being attached to any particular class—his accent puts the natives at rest. It is easier for him to avoid local attitudes and prejudices. He looks at the whole, first, as a game, and then, should he be serious, as an entire human situation. If he cares about it, he develops a calm and attentive eye, a taste for local food, and a passionate dispassion.

•

"Ah, but, being a foreigner, you cannot possibly know what it is like for us. You cannot suffer." But unless one wants to submerge, to become more English than the English, more German than the Germans, one does know what it is like; and one does suffer. The expatriate settles in a country for peripheral reasons; his involvement is with back home. The foreigner's involvement is with where he is. He has no other home. There is no secret landscape claiming him, no roots tugging at him. He is, if you like, properly lost, and so in a position to rediscover the world, from the outside in.

•

To be lost, it is not necessary to inhabit a wilderness, nor even to cry.

•

Belonging. I am not sure what it means, for I think I always resisted it (I still have a crawling terror of being caught in a community singsong). As for families, they are serviceable social units for a certain time only. With luck, the relationships within them will turn into quite ordinary human ones; otherwise they will wither away. If I belonged to anything, it was to the small, but then enormous, landscapes of my childhood, to houses, trees, gardens, walks—only then was my absorption so utter that I felt no separation between myself and an outside world. Childhood landscapes are an entire containment of mystery—we spend a good part of our lives trying to find them again, trying to lose ourselves in the sense in which children are lost. We come away with no more than occasional glimpses, whiffs, suggestions, and yet these are enough, often, to transform suddenly the whole current of our lives. A smell recalls a whole vanished state of being; the sound of a word reaches far back, beyond memory. The beginning of poetry for me was the dazzling realization of all that seemed to be magically compressed into the word "weather."

•

The sense of oddness, of surprise, of amazement. Occupying places, contexts, languages, we grow used to them. Habit sets in, and they cease to astonish us. In a foreign country, this does not happen, for nothing is exactly recognizable; it has not been with us from our beginnings. The architecture is odd, the shops unexpected; the faces provoke curiosity rather than recognition.

And the money—the only real money is the money one knows as a child, for one feels strongly about what it should be worth. Other currencies are play money, coupons; as such, one uses them in a more human, less excruciating way. In a foreign country, the pattern of days is less predictable—each one has its character, and is easier to remember. So, too, the weather; and so, too, the shape and feel of newspapers, the sound of bells, the taste of beer and bread. It is all rather like waking up and not knowing who or where one is. If, instead of simple recognition, one can go through a proper *realization*, then quite ordinary things take on an edge; one keeps discovering oneself miraculously alive. So, the strangeness of a place propels one into life. The foreigner cannot afford to take anything for granted.

•

In a time like this, it becomes more and more difficult to be lost. It is astonishing into what stark, deserted crevices of the world Coca-Cola signs have found their way. But because we have all begun to look, dress, and smell alike, it is still too easy to assume that we are.

•

Language. To alight in a country without knowing a word of the language is a worthwhile lesson. One is reduced, whatever identity or distinction one has achieved elsewhere, to the level of a near-idiot, trying to conjure up a bed in sign language. Instead of eavesdropping drowsily, one is forced to look at the eyes, the gestures, the intent behind the words. One is forced back to a watchful silence.

•

Learning a foreign language is a process of slowly divesting one-self of scaffolding. In the end, something stands up by itself and, if it is lucky, walks away. We lean out desperately to hear how we sound but, alas, we will never know. Not to be able to put oneself into words is the most searing of frustrations; behind the pittering phrases, a huge figure is gesticulating violently. We are suddenly reduced to what we are able to say. And even when we have mastered a language sufficiently well, it keeps trapping us, refusing to allow us to finish a train of thought by deserting us suddenly, making fun of us by coming out wrong. The language we grow up with is our servant; we are always a step ahead of it. A new language, however, already exists; we have to grasp hold of it by the tail, and are never wholly sure where it will take us.

•

How clumsy on the tongue, these acquired idioms,
after the innuendos of our own. How far
we are from foreigners, what faith
we rest in one sentence, hoping a smile will follow
on the appropriate face, always wallowing
between what we long to say and what we can,
trusting the phrase is suitable to the occasion,
the accent passable, the smile real,
always asking the traveller's fearful question—
what is being lost in translation?

Something, to be sure. And yet, to hear
the stumbling of foreign friends, how little we care
for the wreckage of word or tense. How endearing they are,
and how our speech reaches out, like a helping hand,
or limps in sympathy. Easy to understand,
through the tangle of language, the heart behind
groping toward us, to make the translation of
syntax into love.

•

To speak two or three languages is to have two or three totally different selves, like odd suits of clothing. Some fit more easily than others—it is rare to find an American or an Englishman who will speak three languages equally well. As W. H. Auden remarks, "Like all lovers, we are prejudiced; one may love French, or Italian, or Spanish, but one cannot love all three equally." Even so, I am still aware of having, in Spanish (the language I happen to love), a personality entirely different from my English-speaking one—nor is it simply me-in-translation. I realize this most acutely when I listen to a Spanish friend speaking English. He changes before my ears, and I think, How can I possibly sound to him? "If you knew me in English," I say—but of course, it is impossible. Language, if we care about using it well, rather than efficiently, forever separates us. I have often listened to simultaneous translation between two languages I know well. The meaning? Oh yes, the meaning is there; but it is just *not the same experience.*

•

Moving between several languages, however, only dramatizes what happens all the time within our own language: whatever our accent, we do not speak in the same voice to a baby, to a clergyman, to an old friend, to a foreigner. The feeling, the wavelengths, act on our voices and change them. Joyce once remarked, in passing: "Isn't it contradictory to make two men speak Chinese and Japanese respectively in a pub in Phoenix Park, Dublin? Nevertheless, that is a logical and objective method of expressing a deep conflict, an irreducible antagonism." If voices are anything to go by, then the idea of having a fixed, firm self is wildly illusory. We expect those with whom we are in sympathy to listen to what is behind our voice; it is horrifying to have someone listen to nothing more than what we say.

•

What, really, does it mean to speak in one's own voice? Is there such a voice? Possibly, but I doubt whether it would ever coincide with any of the voices or accents we use, either in public or in private. Nor is it the odd, anonymous voice we hear reading poems to us as we sit silently and attentively in front of them. It is something between a movement of the mind and a way with words, a current, an undertow, slightly beneath the surface of our saying. Nobody's voice, but one's own.

•

For a writer, it is an invaluable holiday to speak, in the course of the day, a language other than the one he writes in. When he comes to use his own language, it seems washed and clean. Kraus remarks: "My language is the universal whore whom I have to make into a virgin." For the foreigner, however, his own language remains steadily virginal.

•

Children who are bilingual have no difficulty distinguishing between their languages—they associate them with people, and switch quite simply, according to who speaks what. The main problem for people who are genuinely bi- or trilingual occurs when they come to write in any one of their languages; they are too used to language as a mechanism by then. Unless they have felt language as mystery (as children do when they repeat a word like "boomerang" endlessly, out of delight), they will never be able to convey a like mystery, and stay stranded in silence.

•

Ideally, we may arrive at a point of civilization where everybody speaks his own language, and understands everybody else's. Unfortunately, although this can occasionally happen, it feels unnatural. A nuance, a figure of speech, can only provoke another in the same language. The most untidy conversations are those in which too many people know too many languages; they inevitably get out of control. The English are rigorously unsympathetic to foreigners, being excessively proud of their own language. I will never forget a small, lavender-clad Englishwoman standing over her frail collection of luggage at Barcelona airport, waving her scrawny umbrella in the faces of a voluble host of Spanish officials, and snorting, "I don't speak your beastly language!"

•

Why should we take such an odd pleasure in being taken for a different nationality from our own? Perhaps because we have succeeded in getting away with an impersonation, in shedding our distinguishing marks. Why should that matter? Anonymity is peculiarly appealing to a foreigner; he is always trying to live in a nowhere, in the complex of his present. To be fastened suddenly to his past may displace him. Languages are defiant connections to different worlds; as such, they become pressingly important. Still, there is an age after which one can no longer learn new languages, after which the self cannot be extended without danger. New languages can be disappearances, rather than appearances.

•

To marry across a difference of language is no more dire than to marry across a difference of temperament; but it can certainly add to the complexities. Explanations are rendered impossible. "Ah, but you don't understand" can become very literal.

•

The lineaments of travel. To travel far and often tends to make us experts in anonymity—but never quite, for we always carry too much, prepare for too many eventualities. One bag could have been left behind. We are too afraid of unknowns to ignore them.

•

Airports are the great nowheres of this world; we have made them so. Just as plane trips, be they across oceans or countries, leave nothing to remember but a drone of passing time, so the points of arrival and departure are made to look as alike, as indistinct as possible. Airport restaurants should serve nothing but manna, not tasty but sustaining. The only thing plane trips do for the soul is make it think twice about what it can take with it. Fundamentally, they deceive us by allowing us to travel without a sense of movement.

•

Sea voyages are meat and drink to foreigners, a mixture of delight and despair, a kind of prelude to dying. The prevailing atmosphere is not exactly one of boredom, but of a limbo almost indistinguishable from it. Every ship has its ministering angels, its characters, its messengers of doom—a row of nuns painted to a bench, a woman with performing dogs, a man who can do tricks with toothpicks. Aboard ship, people are removed from either the contexts they have left or the ones they are going to assume; and this affects them in various ways. For some, it is a relief; for others, a deprivation. Some are impelled to tell the story of their lives, because all at once they have no life and must create the illusion of what they have left and what is to come. Others wander endlessly along the polished corridors, through the Bamboo Room, the Aquarium Room, listening to the tock of Ping-Pong, lost. During a sea voyage, a small, artificial community is created, with the intimacy of desperation. One leaves a ship with a flurry of burning addresses, which, five minutes after landing, have already turned to ashes. I once heard of a man who spent an entire Atlantic crossing in the bar, playing chess with himself. It made me unaccountably sad.

•

Trains are for meditation, for playing out long thought-processes, over and over; we trust them, perhaps because they have no choice but to go where they are going. Nowadays, however, they smack of a dying gentility. To travel by car makes journeys less mysterious, too much a matter of the will. One might as easily sit on a sofa and imagine a passing landscape. I doubt whether any truly absorbing conversation ever took place in a car; they are good only for word games and long, tedious narratives. We have come to regard cars too much as appendages of our bodies and will probably pay for it in the end by losing the use of our legs. We owe to them the cluttering of the landscape, the breakup of villages and towns.

•

Frontiers fascinate us, for, crossing them, we expect to be metamorphosed—and no longer are. Even though the language changes, the landscape does not.

•

Nostalgia: leafing through an old passport on a winter evening, trying to remember what we did from stamp to stamp. M. can remember vividly meals we ate in odd places years ago, beds we slept in, conversations we had. I cannot—my memory is sharper for states of mind, atmospheres, and weather. It is sad to part with a passport—one has been through so much in its company.

•

It is not exactly loneliness that afflicts the foreigner, but more that his oddness and experience keep part of him forever separate from every encounter, every gathering, every conversation. Unless he can bear this and see it as something fruitful, however, then he becomes simply lost, an exile without even a country of origin.

•

Que signifie ce réveil soudain—dans cette chambre obscure—avec les bruits d'une ville tout d'un coup étrangère? Et tout m'est étranger, tout, sans un être à moi, sans un lieu où refermer cette plaie. Que fais-je, à quoi riment ces gestes, ces sourires? Je ne suis pas d'ici—pas d'ailleurs non plus.

*Et le monde n'est plus qu'un paysage inconnu où mon coeur ne trouve
plus d'appuis. Etranger, qui peut savoir ce que ce mot veut dire.*

(CAMUS, in his *Notebooks*)

•

Cafés in Europe. The no-man's-lands where people come to take
refuge from time and from their outside selves, where waiters blink
at anything and understand everything, where people watch one
another silently, across all boundaries and frontiers, from behind
newspapers with indecipherable headlines. A café is a stage set for
an Absolute Nowhere, a pure parenthesis in the swim of time. It
provides somewhere for the body to be while the mind wanders;
and it also provides an infinity of small dramas, a strange polyglot
intermingling of wishes and wavelengths. There, everybody is,
by temperament, a foreigner. And to be a foreigner is not, after
all, a question of domicile, but of temperament.

•

We have weathered so many journeys, and so many forms of
love. Would it have been the same, we ask one another, had we
stayed still, in the mill with the water running under us? There is
no way of knowing.

•

What haunts a foreigner is the thought of always having to move
on, of finding, in the places where he comes to rest, the ghosts he
thought were left behind; or else of losing the sharp edge, the
wry, surprised eye that keeps him extraconscious of things. Even
at his most assured, he tends to keep a bag packed, in case. The
feeling of being lost, however, is never so terrifying when it is
compared with the feeling of being found and dried. It is the state
of falling in love with a woman one does not quite know yet; and
will never quite know.

Foreigners are, if you like, curable romantics. The illusion they
retain, perhaps left over from their mysterious childhood epiph-

NOTES ON BEING A FOREIGNER

anies, is that there might somewhere be a place—and a self—instantly recognizable, into which they will be able to sink with a single, timeless, contented sigh. In the curious region *between* that illusion and the faint terror of being utterly nowhere and anonymous, foreigners live. From there, if they are lucky, they smuggle back occasional undaunted notes, like messages in a bottle, or glimmers from the other side of the mirror.

Digging Up Scotland

I have a friend in Scotland, a painter, who still lives in the fishing town he was born in, grew up in, went to school in, was married in, raised his children in, works in, and clearly intends to die in. I look on him with uncomprehending awe, for although I had much the same origins that he had, born and sprouting in rural Scotland, close to the sea, living more by the agrarian round than by outside time, I had in my head from an early age the firm notion of leaving, long before I knew why or how. Even less did I realize then that I would come to restless rest in a whole slew of places, countries, and languages—the shifting opposite of my rooted friend. Walking with him through his parish, I am aware that the buildings and trees are as familiar to him as his own fingernails; that the people he throws a passing word to he has known, in all their changings, over a span of some fifty years; that he has surrounding him his own history and the history of the place, in memory and image, in language and stone; that his past is ever present to him, whereas my own is lost, shed. He has made his peace with place in a way that to me is, if not unimaginable, at least by now beyond me.

I spent a part of the summer of 1980 digging up Scotland and to some extent coming to terms with it, for although I have gone back to it at odd intervals since I first left it, I have always looked on it more as past than as present. My childhood is enclosed, encapsulated in it somewhere, but the threads that connect me to it have long been ravelled. When I return, however, I realize that the place exists spinally in my life, as a kind of yardstick against which I measure myself through time—a setting against which I can assess more clearly the changes that have taken place in me, and in it. When I go back, I am always trying on the country to see if it still fits, or fits better than it did. In one sense, the place is as comfortable to me as old clothes; in another, it is a suit that did not fit me easily from the beginning.

Still, the landscapes of childhood are irreplaceable, since they have been the backdrops for so many epiphanies, so many realizations. I am acutely aware, in Scotland, of how certain moods of the day will put me suddenly on a sharp edge of attention. They have occurred before, and I experience a time warp, past and present in one, with an intense physicality. That double vision is enough to draw anyone back anywhere, for it is what gives us, acutely, the experience of living *through* time, rather than simply living *in* time. People's faces change when they begin to say, "I once went back to . . ." Something is happening to them, some rich realization, the thrill of retrieval that pervades Nabokov's writing, past and present in one. Places provide these realizations more readily than people do: places have longer lives, for one thing, and they weather in less unpredictable ways. Places are the incarnations of a modus vivendi and the repositories of memory, and so always remain accessible to their own children; but they make very different demands on their inhabitants. In Scotland, the sense of place is strong; when I had left that attachment behind me, I had a loose curiosity about new places, and I still spark up at the notion of going somewhere I have never been to before.

Nevertheless (a favorite Scottish qualification), places embody a consensus of attitudes; and while I lived in a cheerful harmony with the places I grew up in, as places, I did not feel one with them. The natural world and the human world separated early for me. I felt them to be somehow in contradiction, and still do. The Scottish landscape—misty, muted, in constant flux and shift—intrudes its presence in the form of endlessly changing weather; the Scottish character, eroded by a bitter history and a stony morality, and perhaps in reaction to the changing turbu-

lence of weather, subscribes to illusions of permanence, of durability, asking for a kind of submission, an obedience. I felt, from
the beginning, exhilarated by the first, fettered by the second.
Tramps used to stop at our house, men of the road, begging a cup
of tea or an old shirt, and in my mind I was always ready to leave
with them, because between Scotland and myself I saw trouble
ahead.

When I go back to Scotland, I gravitate mostly to the East Neuk
of Fife, that richly farmed promontory jutting into the North Sea
to the northeast of Edinburgh, specifically to the town of St. Andrews, a well-worn place that has persisted in my memory from
the time I first went there, a very young student at a very ancient
university. I have come and gone at intervals over some thirty
years, and St. Andrews has changed less in that time than any
other place I can think of. It is a singular place, with an aura all its
own. For a start, it has a setting unfailingly beautiful to behold in
any weather—the curve of St. Andrews Bay sweeping in from
the estuary of the River Eden across the washed expanse of the
West Sands, backed by the windy green of the golf courses, to the
town itself, spired, castled, and cathedraled, punctuated by irregular bells, cloistered and grave, with gray stone roofed in slate or
red tile, kempt ruins and a tidy harbor, the town backed by green
and gold fields with their stands of ancient trees. If it has the air
of a museum, that is no wonder, for it sits placidly on top of a
horrendous past. From the twelfth century on, it was in effect the
ecclesiastical capital of Scotland, but the Reformation spelled its
downfall: its vast cathedral was sacked, and by the seventeen-hun-
dreds the place had gone into a sad decline. Its history looms
rather grimly, not just in the carefully tended ruins of castle and
cathedral but in the well-walked streets; inset in the cobblestones
at the entrance to St. Salvator's College quadrangle are the initials
"P.H.," for Patrick Hamilton, who was burned as a martyr on
that spot in 1528; students acquire the superstition of never tread-
ing on the initials. With such a weighty past so tangibly present,
the townspeople assume the air and manner of custodians, mak-

ing themselves as comfortable and inconspicuous as they can among the ruins, and turning up their noses at the transients— the students, the golfers, the summer visitors. Yet, as in all such situations, it is the transients who sustain the place, who flock into it, year in, year out, to the present-day shrines of the university and the golf courses.

The date of the founding of the University of St. Andrews is given, variously, as 1411 or 1412: the ambiguity arises from the fact that in fifteenth-century Scotland the year began on March 25, and the group of scholars who founded the institution received their charter in February of that dubious year. Such matters are the stuff of serious controversy in St. Andrews. As students, we felt admitted to a venerable presence, even if the curriculum appeared to have undergone only minimal alteration since 1411. A kind of wise mist enveloped the place, and it seemed that we could not help absorbing it, unwittingly. The professors lectured into space, in an academic trance; we took notes, or borrowed them; the year's work culminated in a series of written examinations on set texts, which a couple of weeks of intense immersion, combined with native cunning and a swift pen, could take care of. What that serious, gravid atmosphere did was to make the present shine, in contradistinction to the past. Tacitly and instinctively, we relished the place more than the dead did or could, and we felt something like an obligation to fly in the face of the doleful past. The green woods and the sea surrounded us, the library, and an ocean of time. When I left St. Andrews to go into the Navy in the Second World War, the place, over my shoulder, took on a never-never aura—not simply the never-neverness of college years but as contrast to the troubled state of the times. It appeared to me, in that regard, somewhat unreal.

In its human dimension, St. Andrews embodied the Scotland I chose to leave behind me. The spirit of Calvin, far from dead, stalked the countryside, ever present in a pinched wariness, a wringing of the hands. We were taught to expect the worst— miserable sinners, we could not expect more. A rueful doom ruf-

fles the Scottish spirit. It takes various spoken forms. That summer, a man in Edinburgh said to me, "See you tomorrow, if we're
spared," bringing me to a horrified standstill. "Could be worse"
is a regular verbal accolade; and that impassioned cry from the
Scottish spirit "It's no' right!" declares drastically that *nothing* is
right, nothing will ever be right—a cry of doom. Once at an international rugby match between Scotland and England in which
the Scots, expected to win comfortably, doggedly snatched defeat
from the jaws of victory, a friend of mine noticed two fans unroll
a carefully prepared, hand-stitched banner bearing the legend
"WE WUZ ROBBED." The wariness is deep-rooted. I prize the encounter I once had with a local woman on the edge of St. Andrews, on a heady spring day. I exclaimed my pleasure in the day,
at which she darkened and muttered, "We'll pay for it, we'll pay
for it"—a poem in itself.

> It was a day peculiar to this piece of the planet,
> when larks rose on long thin strings of singing
> and the air shifted with the shimmer of actual angels.
> Greenness entered the body. The grasses
> shivered with presences, and sunlight
> stayed like a halo on hair and heather and hills.
> Walking into town, I saw, in a radiant raincoat,
> the woman from the fish-shop. "What a day it is!"
> cried I, like a sunstruck madman.
> And what did she have to say for it?
> Her brow grew bleak, her ancestors raged in their graves
> as she spoke with their ancient misery:
> "We'll pay for it, we'll pay for it, we'll pay for it!"

And my father, who gleefully collected nuggets of utterance,
often told of an old parishioner of his who, in the course of a
meeting, rose to his feet and declared, "Oh, no, Mr. Reid. We've
tried change, and we know it doesn't work." I noticed on a bus I
caught in St. Andrews on my last visit, a sign that read "PLEASE

LOWER YOUR HEAD"—a piece of practical advice that had, for me, immediate Calvinist overtones.

Some of that girn and grumble lingers on in the Scots. The choice is to succumb to it or to struggle energetically against it. Or, of course, to leave it behind—the woe and the drear weather—and begin again in kinder climates. What Calvin ingrained in the Scottish spirit was an enduring dualism. "The Strange Case of Dr. Jekyll and Mr. Hyde" is the quintessential Scottish novel. The mysterious elixir of transformation is simply whisky, which quite often turns soft-spoken Scots into ranting madmen. Mr. Hyde lurks in these silent depths. Virtue had to be achieved at the expense of the flesh and the physical world, in which we were always being judged and found wanting—the world, it seemed, had a vast, invisible scoreboard that gave no marks for virtue but buzzed mercilessly at miscreants. It buzzed for me. It buzzed for me and for Kathleen, one of my sisters, so regularly that we became renegades, outwitting the system when we could. In St. Andrews, that dreich outlook regularly took the form of an audible sniff of disapproval.

I was born in rural Scotland, in Galloway, in the warm southwest, a gentle, kindly beginning, for we were bound by the rhythms of the soil, always outdoors, helping at neighboring farms, haunting small harbors, looking after animals, or romping in the oat and barley fields that lay between our house and the sea. My father was a country minister, my mother a doctor. Summers, we shifted to the island of Arran: fish, mountains, and green fields. My father's parish had upward of seven hundred souls, in the village and on the surrounding farms, and, as often as not, my parents' stipends would come in the form of oats, potatoes, eggs, and game. When my father, from the pulpit, read of "a land flowing with milk and honey," I was overcome by the beauty of the image, and had no doubt at all that he was talking about where we lived, for one of my chores was to fetch from the rich-smelling creamery across the fields a pitcher of milk still warm from the evening milking; the honey my father drew, with our wary help, from the hive at the end of the garden. When we eventually left Galloway for the flintier east, a glass closed over that time, that landscape. We had left the garden behind, and how it glowed, over our shoulders, how it shined!

The peopled world, as I grew into it from then on, seemed to me to take the form of an intricate network of rules designed to curb any spontaneous outbreak of joy or pleasure. The black cloud of Calvin that still hung over the Scottish spirit warned us from the beginning that our very existence was somehow unfortunate, gratuitous; that to be conspicuous through anything other than self-effacing virtue amounted to anarchy. A God-fearing people—but the emphasis lay on the fearing. When I first took my son to Scotland, he asked me after only a few days, "Papa, why are the people always saying they are sorry? What are they sorry about?" About their very existences, for they are forever cleaning and tidying, as though to remove all trace of their presence, as though bent on attaining anonymity. Nothing short of submission was expected. It seemed to me that the human world ran on a kind of moral economics, entirely preoccupied with judging and keeping score, while in the natural world I saw harmonies everywhere, I saw flux and change, but I saw no sharp duality. The two worlds were out of key.

A college friend of mine who later practiced as a psychiatrist in Edinburgh was fond of saying that if Freud had known anything about Scotland he would have left Vienna like an arrow and taken on the whole population as a collective patient, to treat the national neurosis, the compulsive-obsessive rigidity that permeates its population. Yet as I look back on my childhood's cast of characters I am always amazed at what wild eccentricities the society accommodated, given its stern center—what aberrant madnesses it managed to domesticate. It did so by marking out certain wilder souls as "characters," thereby banishing them to glass bubbles of their own, and rendering them harmless. When I bring some of them to mind now—Pim the Poacher, who tracked down empty bottles all over the countryside and filled his cottage with them, all but one small room; Sober John, who read aloud from old newspapers in the marketplace—I realize that the people of the town unwittingly kept these poor souls safe by wrapping them in kindness. (A sort of impartial kindness prevails in Scotland, keeping stronger emotions in check—the kindness that takes the form of an immediate cup of tea for the distressed.) But the turning of certain individuals into "characters" was also used to take care of dissident prophets and critics—anybody who threatened the unanimous surface of things. Similarly, at the University of St. Andrews, dissenting students, if heard at all, were listened to with a tolerant, kindly half smile. ("Thank you. And now shall we return to the text?") Such a society must inevitably generate renegades, and Scotland has always done so, in droves—those renegades who turn up all over the world, not just as ship's engineers but in almost every outpost of civilization, where the cardinal Scottish virtue of self-sufficiency stands them in good stead.

There is also, I think, a geographical explanation for the steady exodus of the Scots over the years from their wizened little country. Scotland is an outpost—the end of the line. It is fastened to England, true, but not by any affection. The union—first of the Scottish and English crowns, in 1603, and then of Parliaments, in 1707—created an entity, Great Britain, that has never really taken, in any deep sense. To the native fury of the Scots, the English refer to everything as English rather than British, and the fact that London, the capital, lies to the south is a constant source of irritation. The Scots' resentment of the English is aggravated by the fact that the English appear not to resent them back but treat Scotland as a remote region, whereas it remains, culturally, a separate country. But the sense of being on the receiving end, of living in a country that does not have much of a hand in its own destiny, causes a lot of Scottish eyes to narrow and turn to the horizon, and sends a lot of Scots in unlikely directions, the homeland a far green, rainy blur in their memory.

I had no such coherent notions, however, when I made up my

mind to leave, for I must have been no more than seven at the time. Nor was it a decision as much as a bright possibility I kept in my head. We had been visited by a remote uncle, Willie Darling, who had gone to live in Christmas Island as a consulting engineer, and who spent his week with us illuminating that place with endless stories, pulling creased photographs from his wallet, reciting the names of exotic fruits as we struggled through our salt porridge. What dawned on me then, piercingly, was that ways of living, ways of thinking were *human* constructs, that they could, and did, vary wildly, that the imperatives the Scots had accepted were by no means absolute imperatives (except for them), that the outside world must contain a vast anthology of ways of being, like alternative solutions to a fundamental problem. As that realization took root in me, I was already distancing myself from Scotland—at least, from its more forbidding aspects. I had no idea at all about where I wanted to go, or how, or anything like that—only that I would. And I did.

St. Andrews turned out to be my point of departure. I left it after a brief first year to go into the Navy, and by the time I got back, after the end of the Second World War, I had seen the Mediterranean, the Red Sea, the Indian Ocean, and enough ports of call, enough human variety, to make St. Andrews seem small and querulous. Yet the allure still hung over it, and I felt it still—felt the place to be, especially in the wake of the war years, something of an oasis. I have come and gone countless times since, returning, perhaps, because its citizens can be relied on to maintain it in as much the same order as is humanly possible. (In every town in Scotland, you will find houses occupied by near-invisible people whose sole function seems to be to maintain the house and garden in immaculate condition, as unobtrusively as they can. In New Galloway once, I watched a woman scrubbing the public sidewalk in front of her house with soap and water on two occasions during the day. She may have done it oftener, but I did not feel like extending my vigil.) The presence of the university and the golfing shrines has allowed St. Andrews to preserve a kind of feudal structure: the university, being residential, houses and feeds its students, administers and staffs itself, and so provides a pyramid of work for the town, as does golf, whose faithful pilgrims keep hotels, caddies, and sellers of repainted golf balls in business. Others retire there, to its Peter Pan-like permanence, bringing their savings with them. As a result, the place has a bookish, well-to-do air, a kind of leisured aloofness this side of smug. I liked to imagine the wide cobbled center of Market Street set with tables with red-checked tablecloths, between the Star Hotel and the Cross Keys, crisscrossed with singing waiters—Italians or, better, Brazilians, carrying laden trays, sambaing, animating the place, rescuing it from its prim residents, forever hurrying home close to the old stone walls, eyes down, like nuns.

I do not think of the academy
in the whirl of days. It does not change. I do.
The place hangs in my past like an engraving.
I went back once to lay a wreath on it,
and met discarded selves I scarcely knew.

It has a lingering aura, leather bindings,
a smell of varnish and formaldehyde,
a certain dusty holiness in the cloisters.
We used to race our horses on the sand
away from it, manes flying, breathing hard.

Trailing to the library of an afternoon,
we saw the ivy crawling underneath
the labyrinthine bars on the window ledges.
I remember the thin librarian's look of hate
as we left book holes in her shelves, like missing teeth.

On evenings doomed by bells, we felt the sea
creep up, we heard the temperamental gulls
wheeling in clouds about the kneeworn chapel.
They keened on the knifing wind like student souls.
Yet we would dent the stones with our own footfalls.

Students still populate the place, bright starlings,
their notebooks filled with scribbled parrot-answers
to questions they unravel every evening

in lamplit pools of spreading argument.
They slash the air with theory, like fencers.

Where is the small, damp-browed professor now?
Students have pushed him out to sea in a boat
of lecture-notes. Look, he bursts into flame!
How glorious a going for one whose words
had never struck a spark on the whale-road.

And you will find retainers at their posts,
wearing their suits of age, brass buttons, flannel,
patrolling lawns they crop with careful scissors.
They still will be in silver-haired attendance
to draw lines through our entries in the annals.

It is illusion, the academy.
In truth, the ideal talking-place to die.
Only the landscape keeps a sense of growing.
The towers are floating on a shifting sea.
You did not tell the truth there, nor did I.

Think of the process—moments becoming poems
which stiffen into books in the library,
and later, lectures, books about the books,
footnotes and dates, a stone obituary.
Do you wonder that I shun the academy?

It anticipates my dying, turns to stone
too quickly for my taste. It is a language
nobody speaks, refined to ritual:
the precise writing on the blackboard wall,
the drone of requiem in the lecture hall.

I do not think much of the academy
in the drift of days. It does not change. I do.
This poem will occupy the library
but I will not. I have not done with doing.
I did not know the truth there, nor did you.

•

When the war and the University of St. Andrews were behind me, I did begin to live what looks in retrospect like a very itinerant existence. But there is a certain obfuscatory confusion in the vocabulary: people used to ask me why I travelled so much, and I used to say emphatically that I did not in fact travel any more than was essential—what I did was live in a number of different places, a number of different countries, a number of different languages. Writing is about the most portable profession there is, yet sometimes it seemed to me that I was bent on proving this to be so by turning my curiosity into a kind of imperative to go off and write about places that had whetted my interest. I grew used to being a foreigner, but I chose to see it as a positive condition, as opposed to that of the tourist and the exile, who are connected by an elastic thread to somewhere else, who talk of "going home"—a thing I never did. Disclaiming my roots, I elected instead not rootlessness, since that implies a lack, a degree of unanchored attention, but a deliberate, chosen strangeness. I felt the whole notion of roots to be something of a distorting metaphor, applicable only in certain rural contexts, like the village I began in. What I was replacing a sense of roots with, I felt, was a deliberate adaptability. I became enmeshed in the places I lived in. The absorbing present seemed to me all there was, and I acquired a kind of windshield wiper attached to my attention, clearing each day of its antecedents.

It was at this point, in the early fifties, that I stumbled on Spain—not by design, since I knew not a word of the language, or by any particular impulse the other side of sheer curiosity. From my first chance landing there, I was drawn in by a certain human rhythm, a temper that, the longer I lived there, I felt to be an antidote to my frowned-on beginnings, to the earlier wringing of hands. There is a frank humanity to Spaniards that makes them accepting of, perhaps even delighted by, their own paradoxical natures. Gravity gives way to gaiety, fatefulness is leavened by a vivid sense of the present. The people in the village we lived in in Spain had a way of standing on their own ground, unperturbed, unafraid, "listening to themselves living," as Gerald Brenan put it. They all seemed to me to be Don Quixote and Sancho Panza in one. They enjoyed occupying their own skins. They had achieved human imperviousness. V. S. Pritchett once wrote of "the Spanish gift for discovering every day how much less of everything, material, intellectual, and spiritual, one can live on"—a quality that appealed to me. And as I moved into the language more and more, I felt altered by it. To enter another language is to assume much more than a vocabulary and a manner; it is to assume a whole implied way of being. In English, if I get angry I tend to become tall, thin, tight-lipped; in Spanish, I spray anger around the room in word showers. Spanish, as a language, demands much more projection than English does. Hands and body become parts of speech. And then, of course, I began to read, discovering a whole abundance of literature that had been nothing more than a vague rumor in my mind. Spanish is quite an easy language to enter on the kitchen, or shopping, level. Beyond that, it grows as complex and subtle, in shading and tone, as any language does in its upper reaches. When I first met Spanish writers, I felt infinitely foolish at being able to utter no more than rudimentary observations, and I burrowed into the books they gave me, occasionally translating a poem, out of nothing more than zest. Translating was something that came to intrude more and more into my life, not so much out of intention as out of reading enthusiasm. But I felt in those first years in Spain that I was growing another self, separate and differently articulate. That experience was liberating, just as my first arrival in the United States had been—liberating in its openness and fluidity, as it is to all British people except those who cling excruciatingly to their meticulous, class-ridden origins.

I would go back to Scotland now and then, mostly in passing. It had receded in my attention, and I gave no thought to returning other than to reattach, in a fairly spectral sense, my irregular thread to the web of family. The point of going *back*, as I still said then, seemed an ever-diminishing one. People from my father's village, staunch citizens of St. Andrews, members of my family, even, would fix me with a wary eye and say, "You've been Away." I could feel the capital *A* of "Away" as a dismissal, a deliberate uninterest, and I conditioned myself to listen to the running account of local woes that followed. I would hardly have thought of referring to those occasions as joyous homecomings, although they had their revelations, mostly in the wet, soft, weather-stained landscape. They were nods in the direction of my origins, not much more. Scotland had become one of a number of countries with which I was comfortably familiar. I came across a poem by the Mexican poet José Emilio Pacheco, while I was translating a book of his, that so coincided with a poem I might myself have written that while I was translating it I felt I was writing the original. Here is my version:

> I do not love my country. Its abstract splendor
> is beyond my grasp.
> But (although it sounds bad) I would give my life
> for ten places in it, for certain people,
> seaports, pinewoods, castles,
> a run-down city, gray, grotesque,
> various figures from its history,
> mountains
> (and three or four rivers).

It was not long ago that my friend John Coleman pointed out to me the Spanish word *escueto*, deriving from the Latin *scotus*, a Scot. In present Spanish usage, it means "spare," "undecorated," "stark"; but when we eventually looked it up in Corominas' etymological dictionary we found that Corominas had an extensive commentary on it, remarking at one point: "[the word] seems to have been applied to men who travelled freely, impelled by the practice of going on pilgrimages, very common among the Scots"; and he gives the meanings of "free," "uncomplicated," "unencumbered," and "without luggage." The pilgrims obviously travelled light, probably with a small sack of oatmeal for sustenance.

The word absorbed me, for it is clearly a *Spanish* notion, or translation, of the Scottish character—a view from outside, which chooses to interpret Scottish frugality as a freedom rather than a restraint. It was just the word for the transition I was then making. In Scotland, I had felt cumbered; in Spain, I was learning to be *escueto*, unencumbered.

•

In July of 1980, I returned to Scotland with a more specific purpose than I had had on innumerable previous visits: namely, to meet certain friends and dig up a small plastic box—a time capsule—we had buried there some nine years before.

•

By an accident of circumstance, I brought up my son, Jasper, by myself from roughly his fourth birthday on. Our existence together continued itinerant—houses, countries, schools strung on it like beads on a chain. We invented a way of life that could not have a design to it, for we had no points of reference. At certain times, pretexts for moving somewhere else arrived, and we grew to accept these as omens. Spanish was Jasper's first language. Born in Madrid on August 9, 1959, he missed by about seven babies being the two-millionth inhabitant of Madrid, whose population now exceeds three and a half million. We rented an old house in Palma de Mallorca from Anthony Kerrigan, the translator—a house in which Gertrude Stein had spent a winter, we all later discovered, a steep, cool old house with a persimmon tree, close to a *parvulario*, where Jasper first went to school, in a blue smock, as Spanish children all did then. Waiting for him at the end of the day, I would hear fluting Spanish voices telling alphabets and numbers, an awe of first school in their voices. We moved for a year to New York, where I would walk Jasper to school in Greenwich Village and gain a new sense of the city through his eyes. But my father had been seriously ill, and though he had recovered, I had the feeling of wanting to be within range

34

of him, so we sailed to London, and eventually came to rest in a houseboat on the Thames, moored with a colony of other boats along Chelsea Reach. There we floated for the next three years. Jasper walked to a Chelsea school along the Embankment, and would report sightings from the murky Thames—once a dead pig, floating trotters up. We took the train to Scotland some-times—that northward transition in which the towns gradually shed decoration and grow starker, stonier, the landscape less peo-pled. The boat felt to us like a good compromise—we could in theory cast off, though our boat, an eighty-foot Thames barge, would, once out of its mud bed, have gone wallowing down in midriver.

Flist, we called the boat—a Scottish word that means a flash of lightning, of wit, a spark. Many friends came to visit, some of them out of sheer watery curiosity. The boat rose and fell on the tide twice a day, and, with visitors, we would wait for the mo-ment when it shivered afloat, for they would stop, look into their drinks, look around as though they had been nudged by some-thing inexplicable. I was translating some of the work of Pablo Neruda at the time, and when he came to London he took our boat in with a crow of delight and ensconced himself there. He held his birthday party on the boat, a materializing of Chileans, and we had to fish from the river a Ukrainian poet, turned to mudman on our stern. Neruda surprised me on that occasion by insisting that the company return at noon the following day, without fail—not exactly a normal English social procedure. As they straggled in, he handed each one a diplomatic glass of Chil-ean wine, and the party began all over again. At one point, Neru-da took me aside. "Alastair, you must understand, in your coun-try people telephone, probably, to apologize for something they said or did; but we Chileans, we have learned to forgive ourselves everything, everything." I felt he was giving me cultural abso-lution.

The existence of the houseboat fleet was always being threat-ened by some authority: in the eyes of houseowners and solid

citizens, there was something raffish, gypsylike, about our floating community, and we held occasional impassioned meetings,
vociferously bent on repelling boarders. Yet on weekday mornings from certain hatches would emerge some of our number,
bowler-hatted and umbrellaed, bound for the City. Jasper and I
became enmeshed in the life of the river, however, and lived as
though with our backs to London.

•

I often wondered about our shifting, our moving, and would
sometimes bring it up with Jasper, obliquely, at odd moments. I
worried about its effect on him, but the signs were that he travelled well. He felt no particular fear about changing places, and
instead had become adept at taking on languages and mannerisms. Moving had sharpened his memory, and he would astonish
me at times by his recall. He could evoke sounds, atmospheres,
houses in precise detail. If I had told him we were going to Bang-
kok for a while, he would have immediately looked it up in the
atlas, without alarm. I had to remember that in one sense he
looked on places like London and Scotland and New York as foreign and strange, familiar though they were to me; but strangeness did not carry the aura of alarm to him—more the sense of
another language, another way of being. I would concern myself
with *his* feeling of rootlessness, only to realize that for him roots
had little meaning. Not belonging to any one place, to any one
context, he was in a sense afloat, and felt free to explore, to
choose, to fit in or not—a freedom that in the long run made for
a cool view. He did—and, I think, does—have a more intense
sense of himself in Spain than in any other country. I had bought
a small mountain retreat there in the early sixties, and although
we did not go back to it with any calculable regularity, I saw how
he lightened up whenever we did go. It was the only continuing
past he had, and the villagers never failed to tell him how much
he had grown, providing in general the trappings of childhood
that our travelling life otherwise denied him. The house in Spain,

however ghostly and remote it seemed to us from afar, served as the only fixed point in our existence. It was there that we took what we wanted to save—a kind of filing cabinet containing the keepsakes from other lives.

Our wandering life did impose certain restrictions: we could not, for example, have pets, because we moved in and out of the United Kingdom with such unpredictable regularity that the obligatory quarantine would have made them seem like children at boarding school. We had a more Hispanic attitude toward animals, looking on them as semidomestic creatures, whereas many of the English clearly prefer them to their fellows.

•

Inevitably—although there was nothing really inevitable about it—we moved. An invitation winged in to the houseboat one day from Antioch College, in Yellow Springs, Ohio (hard to find in the atlas), to teach for a year, and I accepted. We sold Flist, with many regrets and backward looks, and eventually shifted ourselves to a landscape new to both of us. The year was 1969, and the campus teemed and seethed; Kent State lay only two hundred miles away. Heralds came back from Woodstock with dirty, shining faces; no argument that year was less than elemental. At Antioch, we formed friendships that have lasted both vividly and ubiquitously; it was a year of fire, of passionate rethinking. Jasper trudged to a Yellow Springs school, and grew another American self, tempered by occasional nostalgic conversations and leavened by *The Whole Earth Catalog*, the handbook of the times. We had little idea of where we were going to go next, except to Scotland to visit my father, who was going to be eighty. So when the year ended we flew to Paris on a charter plane full of Antioch students chattering like missionaries, and wended our way north. To my relief, Jasper looked on Scotland as something of a comic opera, and I got glimpses of it through his eyes. He found its formality odd and stilted; he endured conversations that might have been scripted in stone. In a certain sense, he acknowledged it as my

37

point of origin, but he made it clear that it was not his by suddenly speaking to me in Spanish in an overstuffed drawing room, out of pure mischief.

That summer of 1970, after spending some days with my father in the douce green Border hills, we took a spontaneous trip to St. Andrews. I cannot quite remember how or when the thought occurred to us, but then, all at once, on whim, we decided to spend the year there. I had some long, slow work to do, and St. Andrews boasted, besides its antiquated university, a venerable Georgian-fronted school called Madras College. On Market Street, I went into a solicitor's office peopled by gnomes and crones, and found that a house I had long known by sight was for rent—a house called Pilmour Cottage, not a cottage at all but an expansive country house, standing all by itself, about a mile from the center of town, in a conspicuous clump of elm, oak, and sycamore trees, screened by an umbrella of resident crows, and facing the sea, some five hundred yards across the golf courses. It looked across at the estuary of the River Eden, on the other side of which lay Leuchars Aerodrome, where I had first taken flying lessons, with the University Air Squadron, during the war, and which had later gone from being a Royal Air Force fighter station to the strategic importance of an advanced NATO interceptor base, manned by Phantoms and Lightnings, and consequently, I imagined, a prime nuclear target—an irony sharpened by those benign surroundings. I rented the house without a second's hesitation, and in no time we were lugging our worldly goods across a sand path that threaded through green golfing sward to take possession of Pilmour Cottage for the next year—about as vast an expanse of future as we allowed ourselves in those travelling years.

Of all the houses we rented, borrowed, occupied, Pilmour Cottage remains, in both Jasper's memory and mine, the warmest, the most ample. It had six bedrooms, a cavernous dining room with a long oak table fit for banquets, and a huge, encompassing kitchen, with a great stove like an altar, where we gathered to keep warm, and where we practiced the breadmaking skills we had acquired at Antioch. The kitchen window looked northeast to sea across the golf courses, and had a window seat where we spent a lot of time gazing. Day in, day out, in all weathers (and Scotland can assemble a greater variety of weathers in a single day than any other country I can think of), there trudged across our kitchen vision an unending plod of golfers, heads bent against ·he wind or frozen in the concentrated attitudes of the game. Jasper, bicycling back from school, would often turn up with a golf ball or two he had found on the path. We looked across at the square stone bulk of the Royal and Ancient Clubhouse, Camelot to all golfers, and we flew kites on the Old Course, their Mecca. It seemed somehow sacrilegious to live on the fringes of a turf whose sacred blades of grass were often clipped and mailed across the world as holy relics and not play golf ourselves; but we never got beyond acquiring a putter, which we would sometimes wield on the empty greens toward sunset, and an old wood, with which we would occasionally drive the lost balls we had accumulated into the whin bushes, to be found over again. The golfers were part of the landscape, like moving tree stumps; but one spring morning we looked out amazed to see the whole course dotted with tartan-bonneted Japanese, who had made their exhausting pilgrimage to play there for one day, and who insisted on photographing us as typical natives.

I looked from my workroom across the expanses of grass, sand, sea, and sky, quite often at the expense of my work, so mesmerizing was that landscape. Wind-bare, sand-edged, with clumps of whin and marram punctuating the expanses of rough fescue grass, the landscape had clearly brought the game of golf into being. The Old Course at St. Andrews has been both cradle and model; other golf courses can be seen as variations on its fundamental setting. The St. Andrews golf courses, four of them in all, are grafted onto the town by way of clubhouses, golf shops, hotels, and wide-windowed bars—an enclosed world through which we passed on bicycles, still clinging to our immunity.

We settled into Pilmour Cottage as though we had lived there forever and would never move. All year long, a succession of friends came to stay, arriving sleepily off the morning train from London and opening their eyes wide when they saw where they were. We explored the countryside, we beachcombed, we sometimes even swam in the chilling North Sea. We wandered into the town and idled in bookstores, the stony town now brightened by the scarlet gowns of the students. Jasper took to saying "Aye!" and soon had the protective coloration of a working Fife accent. One afternoon, we opened the door to a young man named Jeffrey Lerner, an Antioch student whom we had not known in Yellow Springs but who was spending his junior year (improbably, to us) in St. Andrews, reading Scottish history. We all had many friends and turns of mind in common, and Jeff ended up renting a room from us, since we had rooms to spare, even with visitors. The arrangement worked wonderfully well from the start, for I was able to make some necessary trips, leaving Jasper in Jeff's care. Jasper was eleven at the time, Jeff twenty-one and the right cast for a hero, and I felt considerably relieved to have Jeff as an attendant spirit. I went to Spain at the end of the year, briefly, to settle up some matters in the village and to see how the house was weathering. I shivered in the stone house there, bare feet on the tile floor. Scotland was warmer by far, in a winter so balmy that we never once saw snow and throughout which we continued to fly the kites we kept building—elaborate kites, which stood in the hall like ghost figures and which we flew to enormous heights, sometimes even using them to tow our bicycles. Jasper and his school friends took over the outdoors and the trees, tracked through the dunes, and mimicked the crows till they rose in tattered black clouds.

Coincidentally, 1971 was the year Britain changed from its clumsy ancestral coinage to the decimal system. The *Scotsman*, our daily source of Scottish illumination, bristled with angry letters, and on the day of transition Market Street was dotted with dazed locals gazing at handfuls of glistening new change, holding up unfamiliar coins, shaking their heads, sure that the terrible innovation would not last. We hoarded the ponderous old pennies in a jar in the hall, and we had the feeling that the foundations were being shaken for once—that the past was, even in this everyday, metallic form, yielding to the present.

That year, August of 1970 until June of 1971, was the first I had spent in Scotland since I left it, and I found myself taking stock of it—as it, I imagined, was taking stock of me. The Hispanic world irredeemably alters one's notion of time, since it reacts instinctively, existentially, against the imposition of order from outside, particularly the order of the clock, and substitutes human time. Things take as long as they need to, and happen when they must. That had seeped into me sufficiently to make me intensely aware of the orderliness of St. Andrews. Something was always chiming. Punctually at five-thirty in the evening, the streets emptied; shop locks clicked shut almost simultaneously up and down the street. It felt like a place that had taken care to deprive itself of surprises. Jeff, newly translated from the Antioch of the sixties, could not believe the receptive obedience of his fellow students. As we settled into St. Andrews, the outside world grew hazy and remote. St. Andrews had domesticated it, making things predictable, untroubled. Yet I felt that, once again, sitting in the middle of the landscape translating Spanish texts, I was more estranged than ever from the formalities of the place. The presence of Jasper and Jeff, bringing back separate, hilarious stories from school and university, set me sometimes to trying to explain Scotland to them, and in so doing I came to see how little I identified with it at any point. It was the year that "Monty Python" made its first appearance on British television, and in their eyes St. Andrews felt like an endless rerun of the programs.

In April, the Argentine writer Jorge Luis Borges came to visit, on his way to receive an honorary degree from Oxford University. Borges was much affected by being in Scotland, although his blindness denied him the sight of it. He would take walks with Jasper or Jeff, talking intently, and recite Scottish ballads to us round the kitchen table. During the week that Borges spent with us, the official census-taker arrived at our household. The British are most scrupulous about the census, and the census-taker sat himself down at the long dining-room table, calling us in one by one to record not only our existences but a dossier of ancestral detail. Borges; Maria Kodama, his Japanese-Argentine travelling companion; Jasper; Jeff—I have forgotten who else, but I was the only member of the household born in Scotland. As I showed the official out, he turned to me, scratching his head, and said, "I think, Mr. Reid, I'll just put you all down under 'Floating Population.' " He had a point.

My sister Kathleen lived in Cupar, some eight miles inland from us, and in the course of that year Jasper discovered relatives who until then had been only names to him. Kathleen had five children, who formed a rambunctious household—a family that in human energy far exceeded the sum of its parts, for it put out enough to light a small town. Jasper was astonished by his cousins. He gaped at the whole bewildering whirl of family connection. Our own family structure felt tame in comparison—ludicrously simple. The fact of his having been born in Spain made the others peer at him as though he might be an extraterrestrial. The astonishment was mutual, for my sister's children were voluble and full of questions. By now, however, Jasper had grown expert at being a Martian. His three nationalities—Spanish, British, and American—had made him a foreigner in every school class he sat in, and he wore his oddness quite jauntily. He was, I think, ahead of me.

An early spring brought greenness and soft air, carpets of daffodils surrounding the house, larks, hanging invisibly over the golf course, disappeared into song. The days lengthened, and the golfers played late into the long twilight. We discussed building a tetrahedral kite, modelled on one with which Alexander Graham Bell had once lifted a man, and Jasper looked alarmed. He played cricket for the first time in his life, with a certain disbelief. I came one morning upon a gray heron standing in the driveway like an omen, and we gazed at each other for a full ten minutes. Swallows and swifts appeared, strafing the house all day.

42

It was on one of those spring evenings that we decided, on the spur of the moment, to bury the time capsule. I cannot remember who raised the notion or why—it may easily have come from a book one of us had been reading, or simply from whim—but once we had the idea in our heads we scuttled about, gathering up elements of the place we felt to be worthy of encapsulation. We found an opaque plastic box with a tight-fitting lid in the kitchen cupboard, and we poured into it first the jarful of obsolete pennies and then the contents of a box in which we had kept all manner of foreign coins left over from various travels. We got together some photographs and letters, the local paper (the St. Andrews *Citizen*, which we read assiduously every week), other miscellaneous documents, representative talismans that we turned up at short notice. We realized that we had to prepare a note to accompany the scrambled contents, and it was at that stage that Jeff pointed out that burying the box would be fairly absurd unless we expressed an intention to dig it up somewhere along the line. So, casting about for an arbitrary date sufficiently far off in time, we came up with Jasper's twenty-first birthday, August 9, 1980—an occasion so unimaginably far away as to render us helpless with laughter, for then he came up to the height of the stove, and the thought of him tall and grave, with a deep voice, convulsed us all. We packed in the contents, signed our declaration of intent, made some notes on the day and on what we had just had for dinner, then sealed the lid on with epoxy glue. The twilight was deepening into owl-light when we went out bearing the box, a couple of spades, and a lantern lit for the occasion. It had begun to rain lightly as we crossed the front lawn and climbed over the wall into a clump of scrub and rough grass edging the golf course. We decided on that spot because it was public ground, and we wanted the place to be accessible when the time came. A small elm tree stood about twenty feet from the wall, so we chose it as our marker, measuring out an appropriate distance from it, which we all committed to memory, and set to digging. The box was duly buried and the soil restored—with unholy

43

haste and an absence of ritual, because the rain was thickening and the lantern went out in a hiss. We hurried in to get dry, leaving the box behind us in the ground like a knot tied in the past to remind us of something.

Not long after that, a letter came inviting me to Mexico in the fall. It coincided with a vague plan I'd had of spending some time in Latin America, which Jasper had never seen, but with which I was becoming more and more involved, so, after Jasper and I talked about it, after he took a book on Mexico out of the school library and fixed Mexico for himself on his private map, I accepted. I had never raised the question of staying in Scotland, nor had he. Jeff was winding up his year, studying for final exams, making plans—first, to ship out on a French fishing boat, which he did from Lorient, in Brittany, and then to make his way back to Antioch, by way of our house in Spain. The end of spring was crowned by school sports day, the departure of students; my own work was almost finished. When Jeff left, the suspension in which we had lived all year was broken, and we found ourselves back in time. Our lease on Pilmour Cottage would soon be up, and I made plans to go to Spain on the way to Mexico, and once more assembled our worldly goods, dividing what to abandon from what to keep.

There were rituals of passage, leave-takings, last walks, backward looks. We had arrived in and gone from places so often, and seen so many people leave, that we were familiar with all the facets of departing. When the moment came, we took a long look over our shoulders at Pilmour Cottage from the Cupar Road, with a certain quick pang—the house across that low-lying landscape already half hidden in its own elms and pines, the crows hovering. Pilmour Cottage began to dwindle away in an odd kind of smoke. We had already forgotten the box in the ground.

•

For Jasper and me, the summer in Spain quickly became the present—a preoccupying present, because we were putting a new roof on the house there, sleeping, out of necessity, in the ilex forest, and catching up on village matters, changing languages again. Pilmour Cottage had gone into the archives. Certain appendages of it—a wooden spoon, a few golf balls, an etching of St. Andrews someone had given us in farewell—joined the array of keepsakes in the Spanish house. Jasper sometimes mentioned Pilmour, already handling the memory like a momento, a token. We caught a boat from Barcelona to Venezuela in early fall and made our way to Mexico. Jasper attended an international school in Cuernavaca, learning, it seemed to me, not much more than the Mexican national anthem, but that indelibly. We spent some time in Mexico City with the exiled Spanish writer Max Aub, an old mentor of mine—and an inspiring presence, because he was forever inventing imaginary writers, writing their works, and then entering into controversy with them. Late in the year, we took a freighter from Tampico to Buenos Aires, stopping, apparently at the captain's whim, along the South American coast. It was almost Christmas by the time we reached Buenos Aires— the beginning of summer there, which meant that all schools were closed. So during our time there and, later, in Chile—the hopeful Chile of Allende, before things began to fray away—Jasper went schoolless, but he was never at loose ends, for the Chile of those days made St. Andrews (or would have, if we had ever thought of it) more like an invention of ours, a place we had once dreamed up, a place where nothing happened, as different from Chile as was imaginable.

After that long wander, we came to rest in London. It seemed to me imperative that, with such patchwork schooling, Jasper should finish up within one school system, with a semblance of order to it. So he went to school in Highgate and came to terms with England. Apart from irregular sallies to Spain, we stayed put for four years.

Jeff, meanwhile, had finished up at Antioch, had married Nora Newcombe, a redheaded and warm-witted Canadian girl, who had visited us at Pilmour, and who was doing a Ph.D. in psychology at Harvard. We did not see them for a long while, but we wrote when it seemed unforgivable not to. Then the work

Jeff was doing—a Ph.D. thesis on the shifting attitudes toward bereavement in the course and aftermath of the First World War— brought them to London one summer, and we fell excitedly to filling in the missing time. With Nora and Jeff an ease of connection had existed from the very beginning, where we never tired of talking and noticing. The connection they had with Jasper was particularly important in my eyes, and I knew that it was in theirs: they paced his growing, their persistence as recurring friends a matter of great import to him, since he always had so many things to tell them, to ask them, when we met up. We had occasional, surreal, smokily distant conversations about Scotland; but we did not talk about the box.

I went to Scotland off and on from London. My parents grew frailer; my mother died, as emphatically as she had lived; and my father moved between the houses of two of my sisters, where I would go to visit him. On one of these visits, while he was living with Kathleen, I drove over to Pilmour Cottage, took a mooning walk around the house and climbed over the wall to the vicinity of the elm tree. The ground had a thick undergrowth, but I could still feel, at the appropriate distance from the tree as I calculated it, a recognizable hollow, a comfortable sag in the ground.

·

From 1970, five years passed without my coming to the United States—an unimaginable hiatus, for I had been in this country almost every year, or some part of it, since I first came at the end of the forties. I'm not sure now why that hiatus developed, except that we were more European-minded at the time, and that in London friends from New York were always passing through, giving us the illusion of being in touch. I was working, also, through another long scrabble of translation, and I was caught up in the flurry of disaster that followed the coup in Chile—Chileans arriving in London, anxieties of not knowing—and in the obvious withering away of Franco in Spain. In the summer of 1975, however, some pretext arose for my going to the United States, and I decided to take Jasper, since he had not seen any of his American relatives in a long time, let alone the landmarks he remembered. New York felt sunny after London—not literally but humanly. I warmed myself with friends I had not seen in too long. Londoners are scrupulous about one another's privacy, and New York seemed loose and luxurious after the primness of the London years. We did, however, spend those London years in Victoria, a neighborhood that had become the headquarters of Spaniards who had left Spain in those lean times to find work elsewhere in Europe, so I shopped in Spanish at the street market, kept up with the Spanish football scores, and would translate the odd will or document into English for Doña Angelina, who ran a Spanish boardinghouse close to where we lived, and who knew our Spanish village well.

The United States this time had as visibly liberating an effect on Jasper as it had had on me at first gasp. I could see him taking forgotten selves out of the closet and shaking the dust from them. From this vantage point, London seemed suddenly such a polite place—if anything, overcivilized. When I returned to it, in midsummer, it was with a surge of that extra energy I have always absorbed while visiting New York (though not necessarily while living in it). But I returned for a specific purpose; namely, to take my father back to the house he had lived in in the Borders, in order to give my sisters something of a break. Poor old man, he was already tired of his long existence, although he had bright moments. He rested at least half of each thick, green summer day, and again I found myself sitting, alone, in that shifting landscape, writing, wondering, while my father moved closer to dying, too tired, eventually, to say another word. He died as that summer mellowed into September, the way it does in Scotland.

> At summer's succulent end,
> the house is green-stained.
> I reach for my father's hand
>
> and study his ancient nails.
> Feeble-bodied, yet at intervals
> a sweetness appears and prevails.

The heavy-scented night
seems to get at his throat.
It is as if the dark coughed.

In the other rooms of the house,
the furniture stands mumchance.
Age has graved his face.

Cradling his wagged-out chin,
I shave him, feeling bone
stretching the waxed skin.

By his bed, the newspaper lies furled.
He has grown too old
to unfold the world,

which has dwindled to the size of a sheet.
His room has a stillness to it.
I do not call it waiting, but I wait,

anxious in the dark, to see if
the butterfly of his breath
has fluttered clear of death.

There is so much might be said,
dear old man, before I find you dead;
but we have become too separate

now in human time
to unravel all the interim
as your memory goes numb.

But there is no need for you to tell—
no words, no wise counsel,
no talk of dying well.

We have become mostly hands
and voices in your understanding.
The whole household is pending.

I am not ready
to be without your frail and wasted body,
your miscellaneous mind-way,

the faltering vein of your life.
Each evening, I am loath
to leave you to your death.

Nor will I dwell on
the endless, cumulative question
I ask, being your son.

But on any one
of these nights soon,
for you, the dark will not crack with dawn,

and then I will begin
with you that hesitant conversation
going on and on and on.

Jasper finished school in London in 1977, and so we shuttered
up the Victoria flat (which I had rented from Lesley, another sister
of mine) and came to the United States again, I on my way to
Costa Rica, Jasper to find himself a job for a year before going to
college. I had been with him, mostly, for close to fourteen years,
and there were moments at first when I would suddenly feel that
it was time I got home, only to remember that there was no particular reason, no urgency. We were both relieved to separate, I
think, for we needed our own lives, and Jasper seemed quite adept
at running his. Time passed, comings and goings. Nora was ap-
pointed assistant professor of Psychology at Penn State, and she
and Jeff moved there, Jeff still lugging his thesis with him. I went
to Brazil, to England. When I got back to New York, Jasper announced to me that he had been accepted at Yale. We could think
of nothing to do immediately but laugh our heads off.

On New Year's Day of 1980, the day before I left for Puerto
Rico, we had a party at my apartment in Greenwich Village, for
Jeff and Nora were in New York, Jasper had a job in the city over
Christmas, and other friends were stopping by from various
places. Sometime during the day, Jasper, Nora, Jeff, and I found
ourselves sitting round the table practicing writing "1980" on the
white tabletop. It dawned on us all at the same moment, as though

someone had tugged at the knot, that ahead, in summer, lay the box in the ground. We did our share of comic head-shaking and hand-wringing, in the Scottish manner, and then we drew ourselves up, Jasper taller now than we could ever have imagined, and took solemn vows to present ourselves in Scotland in August.

•

In mid-July, I prepared to leave New York, first for London, where I had to see friends, and then for Scotland, because I had not really been back since my father died. I had some work to do in Edinburgh, and I wanted to be sure of having a place to house the others if they turned up. There was a measure of doubt. I could not get hold of Nora and Jeff, who were somewhere in Philadelphia, and all I could do was leave them a message that I was going. Jasper was driving a taxicab in New York, and was rueful, in the way of students, about time and money. We considered for a moment postponing the disinterment until we were all more moneyed and more leisured, and horrified ourselves by the thought. So I left. I passed through London, took the train north once again, and landed in late July at Kathleen's house in Cupar, in the mainstream of a rained-out summer that was causing even the natives to grumble in disgust.

Kathleen and I have always shared an easy dimension. We forgave each other from an early age. She has a marked generosity of spirit, and is never still. To my astonishment, I found myself surrounded this time by great-nieces: my sister's two eldest daughters, Sheelagh and Gillian, had already had seven daughters between them, and there was a little army of knee-high girls whose names I had to learn. Sheelagh and Gillian had both married solicitors, both of whom worked in Cupar, for rival firms; Kathleen's husband, Charlie, was the bank manager. It all felt very dynastic to me, although at times it took on aspects of a Scottish soap opera.

In Scotland, the buying and selling of houses is generally managed through solicitors, and Sheelagh's husband, George Mc-

Quitty, handled such matters with considerable dash. In the course of doing so, he had acquired for himself and his family an imposing pile called Seggie House, built before 1900 for the factor of the paper mill at Guardbridge, four miles from St. Andrews along the Cupar Road. The sprawling house had a separate apartment, which I rented from George and Sheelagh. I had known the house under previous owners, but not as it now was, an anthill of activity. It had ample grounds and stands of trees, it had lawns, it had a huge, walled vegetable garden with a grape-bearing greenhouse, and it even had a tower, with a view of the Eden estuary and the surrounding countryside.

George, stocky, soft-spoken, has a quiet, burning energy, and at Seggie he was turning it to account. From a window, I would see him drive in at the end of a day, in a business suit and tie, and not five minutes later a chain saw or a mower would start up: George, in blue jeans, transformed into farmer. They kept pigs, chickens, geese, and three goats. George felled trees, turned hay, fed animals, rescued children. Everything we ate seemed to come from Seggie; what we left went back to the pigs. Sheelagh, in almost direct contrast to George, has such a vivid electricity to her that she seems to move and talk twice as fast as anyone else, and then she falls back into the repose of a smile. The girls descended in size from Jane, who, rusty-haired and serious, knew everything about "Dallas"; through Kate, moonier and more reticent; and Sara, four, with a piercingly unabashed curiosity; to Kirsty, five months old, who sat on the kitchen table and seemed to be fed by everybody. I never knew who was in the house—or, indeed, where anyone was—except at mealtimes, when they all magically materialized, as the food did. Sheelagh shot off somewhere to teach a class, to take a class, to exchange a child. The growl of the mower signalled that George was back. For me, in that humming establishment, writing felt like an indolent pastime.

I dawdled in Edinburgh—still alluring to me, a walking city. It did look dour, though, after New York. I went in to St. Andrews, called on some friends, bumped into others. They all asked me what I was doing in Scotland. I told the story once, but not again, inventing some other pretext. It suddenly seemed a rather weird story. August arrived. July, according to some accounts, had been the wettest in three hundred years. I had to tell the story of the box to the children, who thought it terrific, except that they doubted Jasper's existence, for they had never seen him to remember.

There is such a deep green to Scotland in midsummer; even in the drizzle, the greenness emerges, and much came back to me as I breathed that summer in. The countryside swelled with growing, and I sometimes drove through the small, neat villages of Fife: Balmullo, Ceres, Crail, Windygates—names my tongue knew well. Talking to George and Sheelagh, I found them cheerfully liberated from the glooms that still hung in my memory, although they were well aware of them. They also appeared relatively unperturbed about matters of money—a change from the frayed days I remembered, when it would have been unthinkable to buy anything without having the actual coin in hand, and when I once asked my father to show me a pound note and he had to go look for one, since he never carried money with him. But then Scotland had badly needed not a generation gap but a generation gulf, and Sheelagh and George certainly had as acute a sense of the world as anybody, brushing aside insularities by ignoring them. They lived a thoughtful rural life—one that was always being translated into activity. On some days, Seggie House seemed as strenuous to me as New York.

I spent Thursday, August 7, in Edinburgh, recording a broadcast for the BBC. I took a train back to Leuchars Junction, the nearest station to Seggie House, and when I got to the house Sheelagh met me in the hall. "Your friends are in the kitchen," she said over her shoulder on her way to feed the chickens. I went through, and there were Jeff and Nora, with children all over them. They had rented a small car and driven up from London. By judicious phone calls, they had traced me to Seggie, but their call had been answered by Mrs. Trail, who helped Sheelagh keep the household back from chaos, and her directions had proved unintelligible. They had had to intuit their way. That same evening, a cable came from Jasper saying he was taking the night plane to London and would call the next morning. We sat in the kitchen and talked, the girls wandering down from sleep on some wild pretext ("I just wanted to ask Alastair something, honestly!"), not wanting to miss anything. Sheelagh filed Jeff and Nora away in some part of the house I don't think I had even seen. There was a thunderstorm that night, and in my sleep I heard the goats bleat.

Jasper called the next morning around breakfast time. He was in London with a friend of his from Yale. They were taking the train up, and, with a change in Edinburgh, would reach Leuchars Junction about eight that evening. Jeff and Nora, both goggle-eyed at being back in Fife, went off to explore St. Andrews, suspending their disbelief. The girls were already enthusiastic about an obvious chance to stay up late. But we kept studiously clear of Pilmour Cottage, as I had done since I arrived. It was for the next day. We drove down at sunset to Leuchars Junction to meet the train, which ground in, salutarily late, and let out Jasper and his friend Allen Damon. We got them into the Mini Jeff and Nora had rented, with some difficulty, for Allen turned out to be six feet five, and intricate human folding was required. We all ended up in the kitchen, eleven of us now, like an assembled freak show, for the sight of Sara standing beside Allen was comical. Jasper had a beard and looked tired. It occurs to me that I have not described Jasper—perhaps because there are for me so many of him, each separate self associated with a particular place, each distinct in my memory. By now, he is about the same height I am, just over six feet; physically, we do not look at all alike, except possibly around the eyes, but we have a wavelength and a language in common, which we fall into very easily. Sheelagh produced food as she always did—less, apparently, by cooking than by willing it into being. We sorted each other out, telling our separate stories, everyone surprised for a time at the presence of everyone else, everyone talking, a stew of accents. At some point, we made an agenda for the following day: we would wake early, dig up the box, bring it back to Seggie, and then make lunch, to which we had invited all the stray members of the voluminous family that seemed to be sprouting with the summer. George had already laid out a selection of spades, shovels, hoes, and picks, and the weather forecast promised a fair day, as they say in Fife.

•

Next morning, we began to materialize in the kitchen about seven—Jasper and Allen last, jet-lagged. Over breakfast, we ordered the day. The five of us would go, taking Jane along with us. George might drop in later if we were not back. We folded ourselves into the Mini and set out for Pilmour Cottage.

There was a new way into Pilmour, past a practice green; a parking area had taken shape where our old imposing gateway had been. But as we shouldered our spades, trudged round the perimeter of bushes, and caught sight of the house, it all swam back, in a trance of time. The house was white and well kept, the grass juicy around it, the trees enveloping, the day, I am glad to say, dry, with a suggestion of sun. Golfers were already out; it was a Saturday morning. I had looked in on Mr. Stewart, the present owner of Pilmour Cottage, at his store in St. Andrews, to tell him sketchily what we would be doing, and he had been quite jovial about our return, promising us extra spades if we needed them. We stood by the wall for a while looking at the house, shifting it back and forth in our heads—all except Allen, who had never seen it before. A sometime golfer in Hawaii, where he came from, he gazed across the Old Course with a player's awe. The morning was warming, and we were in no hurry, except for young Jane, who could not wait to be astonished. So we turned away from the house and found the elm tree, now grown into an adult elm.

It was at this point that a hesitation set in. Jasper, given the privilege, paced off a certain distance from the tree perpendicular to the wall, dug in his heel, and reached for a spade. "No!" Jeff was waving his arms wildly. "You've forgotten. It was three arm spans from the tree." And he started measuring off the spans. But whose arm spans, I asked him. Jasper's? He had been a lot smaller then. Besides, I told them both, I had been back to the site once, and what we had to feel for with our feet was a depression, a sag— as I began to do, in the thick tangle of undergrowth. We agreed, however, to start digging at Jasper's spot and then, if we did not find the box at once, to dig in the places that Jeff and I had picked out as more likely. Well, we did not find the box at once. We dug in a desultory way for about an hour, expecting with every spade thrust to feel a clunk of a kind, a plastic clunk. We found a teacup, unbroken, and a bent spoon. We talked about memory, leaning on our spades. Jeff and Jasper began to recreate the burying of the box, and even on that they began to diverge. Jasper didn't think that it had been raining that night, and hence surmised that the box must be buried deeper, about four feet down. I was sure of the rain, for I remembered the lantern going out. When we could not remember, we grew adamant. Nora and Allen went off to find some coffee, perhaps in the hope that, left to concentrate, we might clarify our collective memory. We did not. Jane pointed out where *she* would have buried a box, and she might well have been right, because although the presence of the house began to remind all three of us of innumerable details of the past, it did not tell us where to dig. A trance set in again for a moment. We dug more. I had broken ground where I thought the box was, although I admitted to feeling promising sags all over the place. My spade clanged against something—a buried can. Nora and Allen came back, and Nora told us about "state-dependent memory," which she elaborated on at some length. It beat digging. Although the presence of Pilmour Cottage was activating our general recall, she explained, we would have to recover the precise mood and emotion surrounding the event to narrow down our memory. But these were nine years behind us now. (She recently sent me an article from the February issue of *American Psychologist* that told me a great deal about state-dependent memory. It is something I have experienced a lot, changing countries. When I go back to somewhere I have previously lived, I put my arms into the sleeves of the place at once, and find that I take on not just its timetable and its eating habits; I also experience moods heavy with dormant memory.) We laid out what we dug up, however, as methodically as archeologists, and we soon had a fair array of objects—more spoons, broken crockery, medicine bottles gummy with mysterious resins, a child's tin toy from nurseries ago.

Then George turned up, having already been to his office and subsequently sawed up a felled tree. (Jeff had earlier suggested altering a road sign near Seggie from "MEN WORKING" to "GEORGE WORKING.") George sized up the scene: we had already dug deepish holes at three points of a triangle of which each side was some eighteen feet long—so widely can memory wander. He asked us a few brief questions, then proceeded to excavate a trench, clearing off the undergrowth with a few cuts of his spade, and digging cleanly down, the walls of his trench exquisitely perpendicular and sharp compared with our molelike burrowings. He made us all tired, but we dug, scraping our way, as it were, toward one another. We leaned on our spades whenever it was decently possible, and looked at one another. It was time to be at Seggie for lunch. Spades shouldered, we stumbled back to the car. My instep hurt.

The children, far from crestfallen, were glad to have their anticipation extenuated. Kathleen arrived, with Charlie, bluff, looking not older but more so, as Jasper said, and Gillian, Fiona, another niece, Roy, her husband—here the canvas gets a bit crowded. But we ate well—salmon that Charlie had caught and smoked, a ham we had dealt for with a neighboring farmer, green abundance from the garden, raspberries that Kathleen had picked that morning. I sat on the step with Jeff a few moments. "Has it occurred to you that this could have a lot of different endings?"

he asked me. It had. The girls had put out on the front lawn a table with a white cloth, to receive the box. We looked at each other, gathered our spades, and got ready to clamber back into the car.

It was at this point that George had a brain wave. A doctor friend of his occasionally repaired electronic equipment, and had, he remembered, tinkered with a metal detector for a fellow who lived on the far side of Cupar. He was on the phone in a flash, and in no time we were speeding to pick up the machine—which had been acquired by its owner, George told me in the car, after his wife threw her wedding ring into a field during an argument. They had not, however, found the ring—an ill omen, I felt. Nor did the machine itself look capable of pinpointing our lost box. We stopped at Seggie to pick up children, for Kate and Sara would not be left out, and neither would anyone else, for that matter, except Charlie, who was already sensibly asleep under a newspaper. We arrived at the site this time like an army, aghast at the chaos we had already created in vain. Jeff and Nora had somehow disappeared, strayed. But we began to dig again while Jane combed the promised ground with the metal detector. After a few excited sorties, we abandoned it, having found that it could not detect even a pile of change we planted no more than six inches down.

George, fortified by lunch, dug off in a new direction. The children pestered us with questions, and we began to feel a little foolish, particularly when a man who was visiting Pilmour Cottage wandered over to the wall. He could not contain his curiosity any longer, he told me, and when I explained what we were doing he looked at me somewhat sorrowfully and wished me luck. The sun was out, the day had turned glorious, Jasper had turned twenty-one, and we had dug up a patch of ground about the size, it seemed to me, of a small midtown office. And where were Jeff and Nora? George, leaning on his spade, looked a bit worn. It was the thought of unproductive labor that was bothering him, I think. It was bothering me. The children had extended our collection of relics considerably, by bringing in odd golf balls and empty bottles from the undergrowth. I hoped they were not losing faith. The clink of golf clubs and the thud of golf balls punctuated the whole day steadily, as golfers, unperturbed by our gypsy encampment, cheerfully hacked their way home. As Kathleen was preparing to remove some children, at a sign of lengthening shadows, Nora and Jeff burst out of the undergrowth, carrying what looked to me like a ray gun with a set of stereo headphones attached. It was a metal detector that looked as if it might have a chance. Jeff wasted no time in beginning to comb the ground with it. Even George cheered up. Nora explained. They had driven into St. Andrews and gone to hardware stores in the hope of renting a metal detector. An ironmonger in Market Street did not have one for rent or for sale—fortunately, for it would have cost about as much as a used car—but he remembered selling one last Christmas to a woman who lived on the far edge of town and whose daughter worked in Hendersons, the booksellers. They had tracked down the girl, got from her her mother's address, driven there, explained (I know not in what form) to the *dueña* of the metal detector—Mrs. Brian, of Schoolbraids Road— and come away with it and more good wishes. At that point, Jeff whooped and jumped up and down, jabbing his finger at the ground. We dug deeper, for Jeff was still gesticulating. Another old can, but this one quite far down, giving us at least a glimmer of faith in the machine. As if to vary our luck, we all took turns, we all jumped up and down, we found seven more rusted cans. Kathleen sagely decided to go back with the baby, but the other children were still glowing, so they stayed. George's face had lengthened like the shadows. Around that time, Jeff and I began passing the metal detector (Adastra, it was called) back and forth between the end of the trench George had dug when he first appeared and the elm tree—closer to the tree. No question, there was an unmistakable hum, a steady hum, a hum that seemed to cover the area of the box as we imagined it. We whistled over Jasper with his spade. He dug, again; again, a bump—and we were on the box. We all stopped. Jasper scraped away the last dirt with his hands, and there it was, less than two feet down, not much more than two feet from the tree. It was slightly split, clearly from the blow of a spade—probably George's first spade cast, we speculated later. We lifted it out carefully and laid it to one side. It was six-fifteen, a golden evening; even the golfers, however, were thinking of going in.

Hilariously, we pitched in to restore a semblance of order to the ground we had combed—with our fingers, it felt. We had to persuade Sara to save only the best of our recovered artifacts. The rest we reburied, leaving the ground as level as we could, to go back to undergrowth. We wound our way to the cars like Millet peasants—tools shouldered, children carried—bound for Seggie. It was going on twilight by the time we got there. We decided to wash off before we got to the box, for none of us were regular diggers and we had managed to cover ourselves with native earth. My instep hurt almost enough for me to limp, but not quite.

When we had assembled ourselves, we moved the box into the dining room and clustered around the table. I had grown curious about the contents, because I had only a vague memory of them. We began to remove them, one at a time. First, however, on top, lay the card we had added at the last minute, before we sealed the box. We read the text aloud. It was full of ironies. "This chest," it said starkly, "containing treasure in coin and various souvenirs of the present moment in St. Andrews in May 1971, is buried here by Jasper Reid, Jeff Lerner, and Alastair Reid, in a spot known to these three persons." George smiled wanly. "It is their intention to return on the ninth day of August, 1980, to meet and disinter the chest in one another's company, and to celebrate their survival with appropriate ceremony. Sunday, May 30, 1971, a hazy day with sea mist, rooks, curry, and kites." And under that were the signatures, mine recognizably the same, Jeff's looking somewhat simplified, Jasper's in large, errant schoolboy handwriting.

We looked at one another. There we all were. We had survived even the digging.

The contents of the box, I am sorry to say, amount to a rather frail memorial of a fleeting time, but we took them out, one by one, dusted them off, and scanned them. Sheelagh spread a blanket on the kitchen floor, and we poured out the coins, the children running their fingers like misers through the mound of huge pennies, at last convinced that we had put in the day to some point. There were three small plastic biplanes that Jasper had reluctantly sacrificed from his toy hoard at the time; there was a photograph of Jeff, Borges, and Jasper taken at the front door of Pilmour, Borges talking, Jeff bending to listen, a miniature Jasper mugging at the camera; there was a postcard of the Old Course with an arrow pointing out Pilmour Cottage, a piece of white quartz, a leather pouch of Jeff's that had not stood the test of time as well as the rest of the contents, a copy of the St. Andrews *Citizen* dated Saturday, May 22, 1971, which we later read aloud. It might have been the current issue: the same civic preoccupations, the same cluster of local detail. There was a pen, which still wrote; there was an envelope from the Chilean Embassy in Paris addressed to me at Pilmour Cottage in Neruda's familiar green handwriting, a history-examination paper of Jeff's, a copy of the St. Andrews *Newsflash*—a small newspaper that Jasper and two of his schoolmates put out, and that ran for, I think, three issues.

There were separate photographs, too, of the three of us, taken roughly at that time. As we passed them round, I grew keenly aware of how differently we must be thinking, Jasper, Jeff, and I, about the piece of time that had passed between our impulsive shovelling of nine years ago and our laborious digging up of that day. For Jasper, it had been transformation—from oven height, happy and puzzled, in the way of children, to full height, a vote, and an independent being. Jeff had gone through the long tunnel of a Ph.D., and had probably changed least, in that he had an early serenity and his curiosity continued as alive as ever. Friendships we formed in the sixties, around that Antioch year, have remained very firm and clear to me, perhaps because, in that vivid time, the talk we had seemed always drastic, it gave off the same

exhilaration that the war years did to the British, it became a de-
fining time, and Jeff and Nora kept that directness alive: they for-
aged for wild plants, they read aloud to each other over the dishes,
they took in the world crisply and intelligently, they thought of
us exactly as we thought of them—as eternal players in a game of
our own devising, fastened together by the habit of making every
meeting into a celebration of that very happening, that moment.
And my nine years? I had written a number of things, gone
through the swirling glooms of translating, but what I think was
most important to me was that after vacillating for so many years
across the Atlantic, a transatlantic creature, I had shifted and had
anchored myself in the Western Hemisphere. New York City is
a good place to be when one has not quite decided just where to
live—although I think that I have chosen looking for such a place
over finding it. Apart from that, I had, as usual, changed every
day.

So much for the contents of the capsule—not exactly a thrilling
anthology of an epoch. But the fact that these inconsequential
elements had lain underground—"all that time," Kate gasped, for
it was longer than her life—certainly excited the children. In fact,
at different times we all knelt round the blanket in the kitchen and
fingered the coins—"the real treasure," as Sara said. The old pennies, some of them bearing the rubbed-down head of Edward
VII or Queen Victoria in profile, seemed to animate us all. We
rose on our knees, crowing from time to time. Fiona swooned
over a twelve-sided threepenny bit from pre-decimal days. Sara
was searching out the biggest and brightest—dinars, half crowns,
and a single Swiss five-franc piece (which she pounced on like a
buccaneer). I mooned over pesetas and duros with the obdurate
profile of feeble Grandfather Franco, whose death we had waited
for so long. I left them to their scrabbling and wandered back to
the dining room. In truth, nothing looked any the worse for nine
years in the earth except Jeff's pouch, which had yielded to green
mold. But it was the card I picked up and fingered—the card on
which we had signed our names to an impossibly distant inten-

tion, opening a long parenthesis in time that the exertions of the day had just closed.

The children were radiant with the occasion, as though for once life had lived up to their expectations. The rest of us were tired enough to fall asleep in the soup. We ate up the delicious remains of lunch, to save it from the pigs, to take in sustenance. We had all kept out a few coins, for sentimental rather than monetary reasons (although I admit to pocketing a sound American quarter, which had not aged beyond the point of negotiability). George seemed to me particularly broody—lugubrious, egg-bound, like the hens. We took a walk outside, he and I, in a night on which enough stars were out to confirm that they still existed.

"What's up?" I asked him.

We paced in the dark, ignoring the goats, the pigs, the chickens, the geese, the hilarity from the kitchen.

"The truth is . . . " I braced myself, for George, when he talks, is nothing if not blunt, emphatic. "The truth is, I thought at the beginning that today was just one of your wild inventions, that kind of playing with realities you quite often do. But, I have to tell you, it has affected me a lot. I went off and sat on a log and had a long think. I even wept at one moment. I began to think about Sheelagh, about the girls, about Seggie. I tell you, my life flashed before me, probably even more than yours did."

I was surprised, but not. George had looked all day like the practical digger, but I had seen that something was going on in the recesses of his being.

"I've decided something," he said. "And I don't think I'll tell the others until tomorrow. But that box of yours moved me a lot. I looked at Rona, the dog, and thought, Well, she certainly won't be here ten years from now. Then I looked at Sheelagh, myself, the children, Seggie, you, everything—heavens, it all seemed so frail and vulnerable that I decided, Tomorrow we're going to bury a capsule of our own. Ten years from now, Janie will be eighteen, Sheelagh and I will be forty, we move at such a rate that we're bound to be somewhere else—I don't mean physically, I mean in how we see things. So I'm going to tell them all tomorrow at breakfast to get things ready for a capsule, and we'll bury it just before sunset. Ten years seems a good time. Sheelagh and I have a twentieth wedding anniversary then, and I know we'll still be married, still misfiring but married, and I just don't want this sense of continuing time to end, I just want there to be another knot waiting in the string for all of us."

I felt warmly toward George at that moment, but even so, I had had my share of time capsules for one day. I suggested we put in things from our capsule. Apart from the card (and what remained of Jeff's leather pouch), everything in it might as well go on in time, as far as I was concerned.

We went in. The children had claimed Allen as a private possession, and he rose to their demands. Allen had surprised us all, arriving as the only stranger at the feast and yet entering in with exuberance and good humor. He patiently pointed out Hawaii to them in the atlas and taught them to pronounce it correctly; he was for them too good to be true, better than "Dallas" (a rerun of which Jane had missed, unperturbed). He became their hero, far more fascinating to them than any of the rest of us—their parents, especially. "Wee Allen," they called him, to their own squeaky delight. We all had our fair share of blisters and aches, and I went off to bed. Jasper came in at some point and sat on the end of my bed, and we talked, drowsily, about the amazement of the day, of arriving after such shifting, such wandering. It was a point of arrival we would remember, a good moment to go to sleep on.

We all turned up in the kitchen the next morning in a fairly desultory order—at least until George came in and told the children what he had in mind. Immediately, they were seized with a kind of capsule fever and went off in all directions to gather treasures worthy of the occasion, piling them in the dining room. Summer had come out for the day—a warm, hazy heat, an enveloping greenness. Jasper looked quite dazed, grinning and shaking his head. Sheelagh shot off somewhere in the car. We interviewed the children with a small tape recorder, asking them what they thought they would be doing ten years from now. Kate said she wanted a baby. Sara, tired of being small, said she wanted to be as tall as Allen. We all added our own adages. George, who had not been about all morning, turned up with a fat sealed envelope and a brooding expression. I cannot imagine what he had written—but then perhaps I can.

The details of the day are blurred; about six, we gathered in the dining room again, and, through a rather painful process of elimination (it had to be made clear to Sara that if she buried her favorite small blanket she would, of course, not have it around), we eventually filled three vast plastic boxes, wrote out the appropriate documents, signed them, sealed everything up. The experience of the previous day had left its mark: we wrapped the boxes in aluminum foil for the metal detectors of the future, and picked out a spot equidistant from three trees—a holly, a chestnut, and a sycamore. George dug a deep, immaculate hole, and we all trooped out, planted the gleaming boxes in the bottom, took stock for a moment, and then shovelled back the dirt, taking turns to tamp the surface level. As the sun was going down, we lit a bonfire over in the grove where the goats lived, and sat about on tree stumps drinking hot chocolate, gazing into the fire, while the goats nuzzled our knees and nibbled at our shoelaces. One by one, the children began to droop and were carried off to bed. Jane looked rapt. I asked her what she was thinking about. "Nothing very much," she said. "But I like best of all being here listening to what people say." The fire began to die, and the dark came down.

•

That's just about it. Such a small event, and yet the ripples from it ran across the pools of our attention, stopped us, affected us. The next day, Jeff, Nora, Allen, Jasper, and I, after returning the metal detector to a delighted Mrs. Brian, took off for a five-day

drive through the places of my past—to the Border country, driz-
zling and dotted with sheep, past the gloomy depths of St. Mary's
Loch, all the way to gentle Galloway, grass-green, smelling of
warm damp, to that village of milk and honey, to the house I was
born in—stopping to see friends on the way. We told the story of
the box in the ground once, maybe twice, and then we stopped,
because it was complete in our minds and it was actually quite
complicated to tell, as I have discovered. I have found that the
telling resembles picking at a loose thread in a piece of whole
cloth—seemingly simple to disentangle but winding in eventually a great intricacy of warp and woof, threads that lead in un-
imagined directions. I did not realize that in digging up that fairly
inconsequential box, that whim of ours, I would be digging up a
great deal more. Significantly, while we were digging that day
away it was the roots that gave us the most trouble. But we cov-
ered them over again, and they will clearly endure. I think, in
fact, that I am done with the metaphor of roots. I prefer that of a
web, a web of people and places, threads of curiosity, wires of
impulse, a network of the people who have cropped up in our
lives, and will always crop up—"the webbed scheme," as Borges
calls it.

There are many threads I did not unravel, many things I
skipped over, inevitably, because I had not intended at all to wind
in the fabric of the past—a precarious dimension, I think, for even
in going over essential pieces of it I realize how much we all edit
what has happened to us, how much we all make acceptable, recountable versions of past events. Mulling them over, as I have
had to do, I find that sometimes the version and the grainy reality
become separated: not contradictory but separated.

I have not spoken of many things. I have not mentioned
money, for example. Living by writing, I had an income over the
years like a fever chart, but there was always work to do, there
was always translating, which I did as a kind of warm-up to the
day's work; there was always enough to keep us going. If we
needed money, I worked hard; if not, I idled. I have not men-

tioned various women, who moved in and out of our lives, who were woven into our existence, shifting, affecting. I have not mentioned solitude, which was an inevitable accompaniment to those years. I used to meet the English writer J. G. Ballard from time to time in London. He had raised his children by himself after the death of his wife, and he once said to me, "Remember, if you are a single father, it's lucky you're a writer, because you can stay home all the time, you have the time for it." He always cheered me up. Nor did I feel so very solitary. Jasper was the best of company. But there was an essential solitude, the *soledad* of García Márquez, or of Melissa in Lawrence Durrell's *Mountolive*: "*Monsieur, je suis devenue la solitude même.*" And I saved, on the bulletin board we set up wherever we came to rest, a clipping from an interview that Truman Capote once gave: "Writers just tend to learn more than other people how to be alone. They learn to be dependent on themselves . . . it just has to be that; there's no way of getting around it." The self-sufficiency was certainly something I had saved from my Scottish past—that and the fact of still having next to no possessions. Although Jasper alleviated that essential solitude, I fear that some of it has settled on him, by unavoidable osmosis.

I say "we" too often when I am talking about Jasper, but I have no intention of implying any unanimity of mind. We functioned as a unit, but for me the whole business of raising children meant teaching them to fly, separately and independently, getting them ready for leaving. I have been much preoccupied by fatherhood, for I felt most close to my own quiet father, and Jasper I have known as well as I know anyone. One moment lives vividly in my remembering. We had travelled up to Scotland during our houseboat days, on a visit, and we descended from the London train in the wan light of early morning, on the platform at St. Boswells, where my father was waiting. The train chuffed off, and, standing in the rising steam, there were the three of us: Jasper, small and eager, my father, pleased and open-eyed, and I, standing between them, father and son at once. That moment dissipated with the steam, and Jasper and I have exchanged the state of being father and son for that of inhabiting our separate solitudes.

And Scotland? It no longer seems a contradiction to me, nor am I inclined to rant about Calvin the way I once did. I have, besides, a stake in its future. On August 7, 1990, I have to be there, Jeff and Nora will certainly be there, Jasper will turn up from who knows where, Allen has promised his presence, Sheelagh will arrive, breathless but in time, George will have the spades ready, and Jane, turned eighteen, Kate, in a totally different shape, little sparky Sara, and Kirsty, who by then will be older than Jane is now—they will be there. Scotland has re-formed itself, in my mind, into the particularities of last summer, a time capsule in itself.

I call Sheelagh on the phone, tell her I am finishing writing the story of the summer. I have in front of me the card we all signed— Jeff, Jasper, and I—and a leaf from the elm tree that sheltered the box, already dried and cracking. A few odds and ends of the story are still lying about, untold. I ask her about the children, the goats, the household. She fires all the news to me.

"When are you coming back?" she asks me suddenly.

"One of these days," I say to her. I might have added, "If we're spared." I do now, but in the nuclear, not the Calvinist sense.

•

The evening I finished writing all this down, at the remove of New York City, resisting the temptation to pick at still another thread, and ready to leave Scotland alone, at least until 1990, I stopped off on the way home for a drink with two old friends, Linda and Aaron Asher.

"What have you been up to?" Aaron asked me, in a misguided moment.

I told him, in the briefest, most encapsulated form.

67

"But didn't you see today's *Times*?" he said, going to fetch it and ripping out the relevant page.

Here is the story in its entirety, page B2, April 24 issue:

It may be the ultimate skyscraper both esthetically and because of its superb construction, but the Empire State Building has not completely withstood the ravages of time.

A time capsule placed in the building's cornerstone on Sept. 9, 1930, by Alfred E. Smith, then former Governor, was removed yesterday in preparation for the building's 50th anniversary celebration next week. The copper box that contained the time capsule was full of water, and most of the contents had been destroyed.

The seams of the box, which evidently had not been properly sealed, had split, according to a spokesman for the building. The pre-cast concrete slab under which the box had rested had not been cemented into place. As a result, all the papers, which included a copy of the *New York Times* of Sept. 9, 1930, pictures relating to the building and paper currency from $1 up to $100—had disintegrated.

In Scotland, enduring is a much graver matter.

•

Afterword

When I finished telling the story of digging up Scotland, I felt as if some ancient, dark creature had risen from my shoulders and flapped its ungainly way over the horizon. When it was published, I heard from lost friends—a bonus from writing. But, although the piece was finished, the flow of time did not stop.

In October of 1982, Sheelagh and George McQuitty sold Seggie House, writing into the deed of sale their right to repossess it for one day, August 7, 1990.

On December 20, 1983, Rona, the McQuittys' dog, died.

On May 14, 1984, Sheelagh McQuitty died, after struggling valiantly against an indefatigable cancer.

On June 9, 1985, Charlie Drummond died, cheerful, in midsentence.

For the rest of us, the other capsule waits, underground.

Hauntings

My memory had always been to me more duffel bag than filing cabinet, but, even so, I have been fairly sure that if I rummaged enough I could come up with what I needed. Lately, though, certain things have caused me to apply my memory deliberately—to a place, a period in my life, to focus on it and recover it alive. One strong reason has been the death of friends, which shocks one through mourning into a ferocity of remembering, starting up a conversation in the memory in order to hear the dead voice talk, see the dead face come alive. The other impulse to put my memory in some kind of order came from a friend of mine with whom I have kept in written touch for thirty-odd years, who showed me a bulge in his ancient address book where he had had to paste in extra pages to contain more than forty permanent addresses for me since 1950, dotted all over Europe, Latin America, the United States. I looked long at them: French street names scrawled vertically in the margins; telephone numbers that rang very distant bells in my head—some of the places grown so faint that I had to focus hard, pluck at frail threads. I have never kept journals, but I have a jumble of old passports, diaries with little more than places and names, and a few cryptic notes meant to be instant sparks to the memory. Of late, I have taken to picking up threads and winding in, room by room, a house in Spain or an apartment in Geneva; then, with growing Nabokovian intensity, the picture above the fireplace, the sound of the front door closing behind. I have pursued my own chronology not so much to record it as to explore it. Remembering a particular house often brings back a predominant mood, a certain weather of the spirit. Sometimes, opening the door of a till-then-forgotten room brought on that involuntary shiver, that awed suspension. These sudden rememberings are gifts to writers, like the taste of the madeleine—for much of writing is simply finding ways of recreating astonishments in words. But as I began to reel in my itinerant past I found that I was much less interested in recording it than in experiencing the sense it gave me of travelling in time, of making tangible a ghostly dimension; for an instance of remembering can, without warning, turn into a present moment, a total possession, a haunting.

Chronology can be a hindrance to remembering well: the assumption that individual lives have a design, a certain progression, persists in everything from obituaries to ear-written biographies of movie stars. A backward look, besides, is usually disposed to give past time a shape, a pattern, a set of explanations. Memory can be an agile and cunning editor; but if we use it instead as an investigative reporter it often turns up conflicting evidence, for we arrive as we age at a set of recountable versions (long and short) of our private time, a set of serviceable maps of the past to replace the yellowed photographs. If I look at my own time chart, it divides cataclysmically into two parts, two contradictory modes of being. The first part, brief but everlasting, embraces the rural permanence I was born into in Scotland, articulated by the seasons, with the easy expectation that harvest followed harvest, that years repeated themselves with minor variations (growing being one of them), a time when I was wholly unaware of an outside world; the second part erupted with the Second World War, which obliterated the predictability of anything and severed all flow, all continuity. When I joined the Royal Navy, in the later years of the war, I was projected abruptly out of Scotland and to sea, on a series of small ships, around the Indian Ocean—endless ports of call that were all astonishments. It was never made clear to us where we were going, except to sea; so I learned to live by sea time, which is as close to a blank present as one can come. I also learned to live portably. We would move, on sudden orders, from ship to shore to ship, and what we could carry we could count on keeping; the rest was in the public domain. My personal possessions were not much more than a notebook or two; and, coming home after the war through the Suez Canal, I watched one of these notebooks slither from my fingers and shimmy its wavering way down in the lime green water. It was my first serious lesson in learning to shrug. When I got free of the service, I went back to Scotland to finish a degree at the University of St. Andrews, and then left, as I had long intended, taking as little as possible and making next to no plans.

Although I passed through Scotland irregularly in the next few decades, finding certain epiphanies in the moods of the place, reconnecting with friends and family, I felt firmly severed from it. It was less the past to me than the point of departure; and, besides, I had long disliked the abiding cloud of Calvinism that kept Scotland muffled, wary, resentful. An obligation of obedience was written into its educational system, which, when it came to imparting information, was certainly thorough, to use one of the Scots' favorite words; but during my school days if we made trouble or persistently misconstrued Greek irregular verbs our extended hand was struck a variable number of times with a thick leather strap, tongued at the end, called a tawse. The last time I was in Scotland, I discovered that the tawse was still in use. Put together a sniff of disapproval, a wringing of hands, a shaking of the head that clearly expects the worst, and you have some idea of how dire Scotland can be. All the other countries I have lived in have seemed comparatively joyful. The gloom, I hoped, would stay in Scotland and not follow me about. Certainly on these visits I felt no pull to stay. I had got used to the feeling of belonging nowhere, of being a foreigner by choice, entering a new country, a new language, in pursuit, almost, of anonymity and impermanence. Scotland seemed to have little to do with my present, and grew dimmer and dimmer in my memory.

In 1949, I first came to the United States, and it felt like immediate liberation. I could sense the wariness in me melt, the native caution dwindle. Fluidity, it seemed to me, had replaced roots, and change fuelled not a wringing of hands but a positive excitement. I taught for a few years, and then decided to live by writing—about the most portable of all occupations, and an always available pretext for travelling. I crossed, and crisscrossed, the Atlantic, mostly by sea, on the great ships that pulled out from the West Side piers in a regular booming of horns; and once crossed under sail. I discovered Spain and the Spanish language, which had far-flung geographical consequences for me, taking me as far as the tip of Chile. I had a number of friends with the same wandering disposition, who would turn up in some of the same places I had stumbled on, and with whom I often crossed paths. What we were all looking for was localities that moved to their own time, unmechanized villages, islands, isolated but not utterly, good places to work in, but with available distraction, refuges, our own versions of a temporary Garden of Eden, which had an illusion of permanence about them, however impermanent the stay. Work would quite often determine my movements; I found that a new place, in the energy of beginning, sharpened the attention. Some of these Edens were remote—a house, a garden, a village, perhaps—and, remembering them, I have to reach far, to remember a previous self. More than that, they are not separate in memory from the people I shared them with. They are places entwined with presences. Looking for temporary Edens is a perpetual lure certainly not confined to writers, who sooner or later discover that the islands of their existence are, in truth, the tops of their desks.

·

I had been back to Scotland quite often on brief visits, to see my parents as they grew old, into their eighties; but somehow I had never dwelt much on how I had got from there to wherever I was at the time. Then I spent the entire summer of 1980 in Scotland, on an escapade with my son and some friends, digging up a plastic box—a time capsule—that we had buried nine years previously, on the fringes of the golf course at St. Andrews. That summer, I spent a lot of time with my sister Kathleen, who had been my great ally in the turbulence of our growing up. Our parents were dead, and we had met only scantily in recent years, but as the deep green summer rained and rained we found ourselves almost involuntarily rummaging in the past as if it were a miscellaneous attic chest, startling ourselves at a remembered name, to a point at which we were mesmerized by remembering. We had photographs and documents that we had saved from clearing up our parents' papers, but we discovered that in the interaction of our memories we had much more. We re-created our parents from the point that we began, not in any systematic way but in flashes, days and seasons in a single vision. The rain watered my memory, and I found my whole abandoned beginning seeping slowly back, even into dreams.

I was born in a village called Whithorn, in the soft southwest of Scotland. It was my beginning; and, reaching back to it, I realize that for me it has remained in a time warp of its own—my personal Eden, in that although it was lost, the aura that comes back with remembering it stems from a time when house, family, garden, village, and friends were all I knew of the world, when everything had the glow of wholeness, when I had no idea of the passing of time except as anticipation. What I have discovered, too, are the contradictions—in many cases, our own mythifications of that time, the recountable, bookshelf version, which we put together to anchor the past in place. Even so, the myth is bound to predominate; we cannot become who we were or lose what we now know.

Whithorn lies close to the tip of one of the southern fingers of the part of Scotland known as Galloway: isolated, seldom visited, closer across the Irish Sea to Northern Ireland than it seems to the rest of Scotland; closer, too, to Ireland in the softness and cadence of its speech. It is rich, low-lying, carefully cultivated dairy country, with a few small fishing ports, and has a douce, mild climate, thanks to the proximity of the Gulf Stream, which has made certain Galloway gardens famous for their exotic transplantings. Whithorn was also a beginning for my parents. My father came from the midlands of Scotland, a member of the large and humorous family of a schoolmaster I never knew. My father had interrupted his divinity studies at Glasgow University to serve as a combatant in the First World War, and had been wounded in the Second Battle of the Somme; had married my mother, who had recently graduated as a doctor from Glasgow University; and had returned, with the war behind him, to pick up his existence. In 1921, he was chosen and ordained as Church of Scotland minister in Whithorn. The church stood on the site of Whithorn Priory, the first Christian settlement in Britain, founded on the arrival of St. Ninian, in the year 397, and a very early place of pilgrimage. It was my father's first charge, a village of some seven hundred, embracing the surrounding farms. My parents firmly took root there, my father healed over from the war, which nevertheless always troubled his memory, my mother had a house to turn into a household, and in later years they always spoke of these beginnings as a lucky time in their lives, for Galloway contains the kindliest of people in all that flinty country—all in all, a good place to begin in.

In shape, Whithorn looks much like a child's drawing of a village: built on a slope, it has a single main street—the houses on each side of it joined in a single façade, no two of them, however, exactly alike—which widens like a mandolin as it descends to a semblance of a square, where the shops cluster, where the bus pulls in. The street narrows again and runs to the bottom end of the village, where, in our day, the creamery and the railway station stood adjacent to each other. Every morning, the miniature beginnings of a train would start out from Whithorn: a wagonful of full milk churns from the creamery destined for Glasgow; a single passenger coach, occasionally carrying those who had business in the outside world. Whithorn was a place easy to learn by heart. All round it lay the farms and, beyond them, infinitely, the sea.

As minister, my father had the gift of the manse to live in (the houses of Scottish ministers are always called manses), and the manse in Whithorn was an outpost, set apart from the village. From the main street, under an old arch bearing Whithorn's coat of arms, a lane led, first, to the small white church that was my father's charge, surrounded by a well-kept graveyard, where we sometimes practiced our reading from the gravestones. The lane continued left past the church, crested a small rise, and ran down, over the trickle of a stream, to the white gates of the manse. A gravel drive led up to the manse, past a long, walled garden on the right; a semicircle of huge elm and beech trees faced the house from across the drive. Behind the house were stables and out- houses, and all around lay green fields. If you trudged across them, careful in summer to skirt the golden edges of standing oats and barley, you reached the sea—an irresistible pilgrimage.

The manse had the quality of certain Scottish houses—a kind of good sense realized in stone, made to last. There were ample rooms: attic rooms, where we children slept, and played on wet days, as we were born in turn; a study for my father, separated from the stepped-down kitchen by a long flagstone corridor, which led, through sculleries and pantries, to the garden. But it is a peopled place, not an empty house, in my memory. My eldest sister, Margaret, was born two years before my parents came to Whithorn; but there, in the house, my sister Kathleen, I, and my younger sister, Lesley, saw the light in that order, so that we be- came a tribe, and fell into the rhythms and ways of the place—a wondrous progression that I took in whole, with wide, unjudg- ing eyes.

Whithorn was not at all well-to-do but thrived, rather, on the comfortable working equilibrium of that countryside. Some of its inhabitants went to sea, fishing, but most farmed; the cream- ery kept the dairy herds profitable; and the place had a kind of self-sufficient cheer that it needed, for it was truly at the end of a long, far line—it and its small seaport village, the Isle of Whithorn, a few miles beyond it, on the coast. There were not many comings and goings, and, so isolated, the people became their own sustenance, and had the warm grace of the countryside. Seven hundred people, if they do not actually know one another, know at least who everyone is. The village had the habit of churchgoing: besides my father, there was a United Free Church minister and a Catholic priest, shepherding even tinier flocks. The three of them became good friends. Like the doctor and the local solicitors, they had essential functions in the community. It was a harmonious place, with no sides, no sharp edges. My birth certificate bears the spidery signature of James J. Colquohoun, the local registrar, who had a head like a shrivelled eagle and wore pince-nez, and who had memorized the local population and its ancestral connections so well that he often greeted people by reciting their family tree to them—or, at least, the lower branches.

The manse, the center of our world, hummed with our own lives. It had the equilibrium that families often arrive at for a time before they break up into individual parts. Our household had its own modes and habits, which were set by the design of our parents' lives. Our parents fascinated us as children—during our growing, in particular—for, separately, they had natures about as opposite as seemed possible to us, yet they were never separate, and were noticeably devoted. My father, soft-spoken, gentle of manner, edging on shy, with a natural kindness and humor never far from his eyes, grew to be much liked in the place. When we walked with him, people would greet him warmly, and we would include ourselves by clutching at him. When we were assembled as a family, at meals, or on fire-circling evenings, he would question us, tease us, tell us stories; at other times he might take us, singly, on visits to farms; but often, poised at his desk reading, or sitting in an armchair with an unfixed gaze, he seemed to have pulled over him a quilt of silence, to be inhabiting an unreachable solitude. We grew used, also, to his different presences. On Sundays, he appeared in the pulpit, wearing his robes and a grave face, and we listened more than anything to the measured cadence of his pulpit voice. After church, except when it was raining, we waited for him in the garden, for he took a shortcut across the fields and dropped over the garden wall, returned from gravity into fatherhood, much to our relief.

My mother revered my father; and, as if to insure his chosen quiet, she forswore the practice of medicine and took over control of the house, the household, and us children, delegating us tasks according to our abilities. As with all houses in the country, there were endless chores, always a need of hands. The Church of Scotland paid its ministers very small stipends indeed, and although the manses were substantial houses, some of the more remote of them had fallen behind in time. We drew all our water from a hand pump—a domestic replica of the village pump—in the scullery off the kitchen. It was the obligation of the last pumper to leave behind three full buckets. The house was heated by coal fires and lit by oil lamps. These I would watch my father assemble on the lamp table, where he filled them, trimmed the wicks, and polished the funnels—a task I apprenticed myself to as soon as I could. We willingly ran on errands to the village like missions—for it was a common practice there to send notes by hand, using the mails only for letters to the world. When my two older sisters were in the village school, I inherited their task of walking across the fields to the creamery with a pitcher, to have it filled with still warm milk, and would wander home slowly by way of my private shrines.

My mother, whose father, younger sister, and brother were all doctors, showed no impulse to practice medicine. I suspect now that, having grown up in a medical household, tied always to one end of a wire of availability, she did not want ours to be so bound. But we got to know the local doctor well, and my mother would stand in for him when he was away, sometimes seeing his patients in the kitchen, which we would unclutter for the occasion. Neither was it uncommon for her to be summoned by an anxious knocking late at night when the doctor was out on call and could not be found. She did not, however, believe in sending out bills for any medical services, and never did. Added to that, my father's stipend was paid in part according to the old Scottish tithing system, whereby farmers who cultivated church land paid a tithe of their crop, or its market value, to help sustain the parish, so we had more than a passing interest in the harvest. As a consequence, our larder, with its long blue slate counter, was regularly replenished with fresh eggs, butter, oats, potatoes, game—the green abundance of that patiently farmed place. My father never carried money, nor did we, unless we were ordered to for something specific. At intervals, he paid all the bills at a stroke, totalling them carefully and going out the next day to the bank to take out the necessary sum. Occasionally, he would let us look at the notes before he paid them over, but I had not grasped the idea of money, and it did not interest us much—except for my sister Margaret, who was already plaguing us with knowing school airs.

My father's single obsession was with cars, and he drove very fast—this always surprised and delighted us—about the countryside, on his pastoral visits, in an ancient Fiat that looked half like a carriage. We had a network of friends on the surrounding farms, some of which were close enough for us, when we reached a certain age, to point ourselves like crows toward them, navigating the fields and stone dikes in between. I loved the days on the farm—the rituals of milking, still by hand; the work that changed according to season and weather—and I used to stay over at one farm, Broughton Mains, for haying in June, and for the golden weeks of harvest in late August: days we passed in the field, helping or playing; days punctuated by the women bringing hampers of food they had spent the morning preparing; the fields orderly at the end of the day, the bound oats in their rows of standing clumps; days that felt like rites. After we had left Whithorn, I would go back to Broughton Mains for the peak of the harvest, immemorially, for there that drama of abundance crowned the whole year.

We spent as much as we could of the daylight of our lives then outdoors, the house a headquarters among the fields and climbable trees, or a shelter on days of rain or raw weather. Sometimes we would be recruited in a body to help in the garden—a string of small bearers, baskets of weeds on our heads. My world at that time embraced five villages, a dozen farms, a river, and three beaches, some houses we visited often, a countable number of friends we knew by name. We sailed sometimes on a fishing boat out of the Isle of Whithorn, and we often watched five or six local boats come in with their catches, sometimes with herring for the taking. My father preached there on odd Sunday evenings, in a small white church that protruded into the harbor, waves sometimes leaving their spray on its latticed windows during the service. Galloway mostly has soft winters and early springs, and we learned and looked for signs of growing, we followed the progress of the garden and the sown fields surrounding us, we eavesdropped on the farms, trying to pick up nuggets of country wisdom, and we practiced looking wisely at the sky.

From quite early on, our household grew its own legislative procedures when it came to deciding the shapes of days. Decisions, serious decisions, it was understood, lay with my father; but my mother was his plenipotentiary, and our initial dealings—from trivial to urgent—took place through her. She drove hard bargains, and sometimes we would waylay my father to appeal her rulings, for he was a natural peacemaker, patient in argument, attentive to language, and, we felt, fair. It was action my mother believed in, and if we wanted to talk to her it generally meant joining her in turning a small chaos of some kind into active order. She, too, had different manifestations. We overheard her at times talking to a patient—certain, quiet, reassuring. My father had a fair number of callers, and she had the skill of a diplomat in seeing that they did not consume his time. But when we wanted to talk to her it might involve holding a skein of wool for her to wind into a ball, or picking gooseberries by the basketful while we plied her with questions, which she answered crisply, her hands never still for a moment.

There is one period that I find comes back to me with particular clarity, but I am also aware of having mythified it: I had barely turned four; Margaret and Kathleen, in the turn of the years, were away all day at school; my sister Lesley, still a baby, slept in her pram most of the time outside the front door, which the swallows that nested in the stables every year swooped past all day long. The days then were my own, and I wandered on a long lead from the house, walking the flat-topped garden wall, damming the stream, skirting the bees, poking in the stables, and gravitating, in between quests, to the house. Outside, I was busy peopling my solitude, but when I came in I would find myself in the flag-stone corridor, the steps down to the kitchen and my mother's domain at one end, the closed door to my father's study at the other. Some days, turning right, I would seek out my mother in the kitchen as she was baking, stocking the larder ahead of our appetites, and I would sit at a corner of the kitchen table, fasci-nated by the soft grain of its worn wood, while my mother, who, although she preferred working company, also liked company while she worked. I always took the opportunity to nudge her with questions, for I was extremely unclear about the obvious differences between the conditions of the visitors who came to see my father and those who on occasion would wait their turn to see my mother. When my father was talking with a parishioner in the front room, all that came through the closed door was a murmur of voices, but when my mother saw patients in the kitchen we heard, more than once, discomfiting cries from that end of the corridor. Were there some people who might call to see *both* my father and my mother? My mother avoided meta-physics, but she would give me occasional small seminars on things like the digestive system, or why we yawn—hardly the whole medical education I was keen to extract from her. Some-times I would go with her on an errand to town, and she would

explain to me who people were, what they did, their names—
teaching me the village and its ways, for she had chosen to live
within its particularities happily and actively, and she was the
source of our tribal energies.

On other days, I would turn left along the corridor, open the
door to my father's study, quietly, as I had learned to do, and find
him at his desk, wreathed in smoke, a pool of concentration. He
always took me in—he had his own quiet, and did not need silence—and sat me on a hassock by the stretch of bookshelves that
held atlases, books with pictures, and an illustrated history of the
First World War. This I would lug out, volume by volume, lying
full length and gazing in incomprehension at the sepia photographs of blighted landscapes and the skeletons of buildings.
Sometimes, when I had his attention, he would begin to explain
the pictures to me, or show me on the map where he had been,
where the battle lines met, but never for very long, for the subject
frayed him. I remember sitting in that room of words and feeling
islanded by not being able to read, for I felt that words were my
father's business—his reading, his sermons, his writings, the fact
that people came to him for his words. Even now, I am still pacing
that corridor.

•

In that encapsulated world, I lived in complete innocence of time,
except that school was looming. I could not think of years as
doing anything other than repeating themselves, nor did I want
them to. But time did intrude, abruptly, into my wide-eyed
world: we left Whithorn. My father accepted a call to a larger
church, in Selkirk—a town in the Border district, much farther
to the east, much larger, with working tweed mills, and set in
rolling, forested sheep-farming country, crossed by rivers like the
Tweed itself, salmon-famous. Needless to say, I had no voice in
the moving, nor did I properly grasp its implications, for I had no
idea what moving meant. I had not, after all, moved anywhere
before. When we did move, time began for me, and Whithorn

became my first loss. After a jolt of dislocation, I found myself in a place I could not recognize, full of strangers, everything to be learned again, and I begged my parents to go back. Bitterly, I mourned for Whithorn, in uncooperative silence, before I began to take a wary look around me. Selkirk was almost ten times as big as the village, and our house had a bigger garden, lawns, a small wood, more and grander rooms, hills to look at, even gaslight. It stood not far from the marketplace, which brimmed with shoppers and gossip; it had a telephone and a constancy of visitors; but I hung back from it, looking bewilderedly backward through the glass that had suddenly slid between me and a place that I had belonged to and that had also belonged to me. Leaving Whithorn was my first experience of acquiring a past; what I had left behind forever, I think, was the certainty of belonging—something I have never felt since.

What kept Whithorn alight and gave it an Edenic cast in my backward vision had to do with the natural world, the agrarian round, a way of life I had seen and felt as whole. From now on, these harmonies gave way to the human world, to other sets of rules and obligations, to a localism we were still strangers to, as we were to the different lilt in the voices. School began for me, and I did not find it an arrangement that I took to, except that I realized that if I were to go through with it I would know how to read at some point, and the books in my father's library would open and talk to me. As children, we were before long occupied in putting together new worlds of our own, making friends, laying down landmarks. In Scotland, the Border towns, ravaged across centuries by skirmishing with the English on both sides of the border, had an aggressive localism to them, something approaching a fortress mentality. Not to be born in Selkirk, we soon found out, amounted to an irremediable flaw; in the eyes of the staunchest locals we were naturally blighted, outsiders by definition—a tag I accepted quite happily, for I had come to much the same verdict about Selkirk.

Whereas Whithorn, with seven hundred people, had been a

particularity, Selkirk, with around six thousand, remained an abstraction. Since it was bigger and much less remote—Edinburgh was not much over an hour away—many more things seemed to happen, and my parents' lives grew brisker; that made them less accidentally accessible to us. My father had a larger study, upstairs, with a window seat from which we could look south to the hazy blue of the Cheviot Hills, where the border with England lay. I laid an early claim to that seat as my reading post, and sometimes, struck book-deaf, I would have to be dragged from it, my eyes forcibly unfixed from the print. A large kitchen on the ground floor became a kind of operations room, which my mother ran just as energetically as she had run the smaller universe of Whithorn. Our household tasks multiplied, and the burden of a bigger garden spoiled my relations with the soil for a considerable time. With several doctors in the town, my mother gave almost no attention to medicine—at least, until the war loomed. My medical curiosity dried up for the time being; but my father, as if suddenly realizing my new literacy, decided to teach me Latin and Greek, for he had been a good classicist. He was patient and enthusiastic at the same time, and I was a diligent pupil, for I felt that these lessons were at last giving me entry into my father's province. When I came to take classics in school, I was well ahead, but I kept the fact secret, because it lightened the burden of the work we were always scrawling away at with inky fingers.

Where Whithorn had been purely a rural community, Selkirk had a different class structure, in part agricultural—a way of life we were in tune with, although after dairy farms I found sheep country dull and somnolent—and in part industrial, for the woollen mills were clustered in the valley along the River Ettrick, at the foot of the town, and sounded their sirens morning and evening. Mill owners, landowners, farm workers, mill workers— the town had an intricate hierarchy. Again, ministers, doctors, lawyers, by dint of their professions, moved easily across those class lines, but the town itself was stiff with them. We found ourselves referred to as the manse children, and a certain expectation of virtue was pinned to us with the phrase. As doctor's children, too, I suppose we were expected to be models of health. My mother was the most downright of doctors, and, I think, suspected the sick mostly of malingering. We certainly could not fool her with imaginary ills; but when she had to doctor one of us with any seriousness we saw her change, as my father did on Sundays, into someone serious and separate from us.

Margaret, my eldest sister, and Lesley, my youngest, formed a kind of parenthesis to our family. It was Kathleen and I, closest in age and temperament, who compared notes, speculated, pooled information; and it was with Kathleen that I shared my perplexities over religion, my father's domain. We were by now used to his transformations from old gardening clothes into the dark formality, clerical collar in place, tile hat in hand, that a wedding or a funeral demanded; but while in Whithorn churchgoing had seemed a cheerful family occasion, in Selkirk the lofty, well-filled church wore a kind of pious self-importance, and churchgoing took on a solemnity we had not bargained for. Saturday nights, we would get out of the way early, leaving my father settled in his study, hunched into the small hours over the bones of his sermon for the next day. On Sundays, he would appear for breakfast already shaved, dressed, and collared, and would set out for church ahead of us, leaving us to ready ourselves for the summoning of the church bell. The manse pew, where we were obliged to sit, was prominently placed, so my mother, who took appearances much more seriously than any of the rest of us, decreed that, barring emergencies like the Great Plague, three of the four of us would attend church with her every Sunday morning—in a rotation we sometimes used as a trading currency. Churchgoing was something I grew used to, letting my mind wander about in an uncontrolled mixture of attentions; but as I took in the bewildering anthology of human faces—I gazed as often as I dared at a man with white hair and a ginger mustache—I was listening in a subliminal way to the cadence of my father's voice, mesmerized by the sudden incandescence of a phrase, fascinated by the convoluted metrics of certain hymns, stirred by the grave measures of the liturgy, aware of language as a kind of spell, and astonished when, freed by a dismissive organ voluntary, the congregation made its way out into the unsanctified air, and all burst out talking at once, as though to make up for the imposed silence of church.

But to be left at home one Sunday out of four, to be alone, with the run of the house—that was the time we coveted. We were obliged only to keep an eye on whatever was simmering on the stove. We were expected to be chiselling away at homework. But the whole house was ours for a church-length, and we could open otherwise forbidden doors, drawers, and books, and play the piano without fear of being heard, although sometimes I would wander slowly from room to room just to take in the rarity of the silence. Everything had to be back in place before the gate clicked and the churchgoers tumbled in, smug with virtue but glad to be freed from the weight of it. Sunday lunches were events. More sumptuous than usual, they awaited my father's return, unrobed and predictably cheerful, for he had cleared what seemed to us his week's work—or, at least, its main hurdle—and the rest of the day lay ahead for us like a gift of time, before Monday dawned.

Kathleen and I at one point befriended Tom the Beadle, the church janitor, and, borrowing his keys, we would sometimes go exploring in the empty church: the halls underneath it, which smelled of musty stone; the cushioned vestry, where my father changed; up the back staircase into the church itself, and into the pulpit, where, however, we did not linger. In time, we learned to start the organ and play whatever scraps of music we had at our fingertips, but we were eventually banished by Tom, who feared, I think, that one day we would be tempted to pull the bell rope— his most public and audible formal duty. I feel that what perplexed us then was the sense, where religion was concerned, of having backstage connections. I realize now that I never felt a religious fervor: for me, the mysteries lay elsewhere. Very clearly, I had worked out the idea that God, in some inexplicable way, was my father's boss, and I saw church services from backstage as weekly programs with minor variations. Besides, my father was much less a religious thinker than an instinctive comforter and clarifier. I knew that he hid his shyness behind an assumed solemnity, and what concerned me most was that his parishioners saw and heard only his grave public self, not the person he changed into when he came back to us, teasing, telling stories, gloom gone. He never laid down laws, nor did we ever discuss religion: questions of doubt or belief did not trouble him, for he was less interested in religious dogma than in its human translation. For him, being a minister implied the same human practicality that was my mother's dimension. We used to suggest to them that they work as a team, but in fact they did just that. It was in his human form that we worshipped our father. His more formal self he left behind in the vestry, with his robes. He forgave us our irreverence—he abhorred piety and did not make us feel any obligation toward virtue. Our family image concerned my mother much more, but our natural anarchy prevailed. Their differences captivated us more and more. My father had infinite patience, my mother very little; and although she was as voluble as he was quiet, she never read, while I had entered a whole universe of reading, and my father would leave books lying about for me to discover. I always read during his sermons, a volume of Oxford *World Classics*, which were luckily bound like Bibles; my father, too shy to let me know that he knew and did not mind, always gave me a new *World Classic* for my birthday. Yet although I had moved into my father's domain of language, I still had a secret fixation on being a doctor—an unmentioned ambition I shelved once the war had begun, for medical students were exempted from military service and I had no wish to be.

Selkirk enclosed us in its rituals, Whithorn receded; and I suppose I began to think of it quite early as my childhood, my lost past, for the connections thinned and the haunting subsided in the frenzy of the present. I now think of that time in Selkirk, when the war loomed, as the beginning of disintegration—a movement from that once-glimpsed wholeness toward a splintering of time, the oncoming of many separations. We would never belong again, in that first sense. In Selkirk, I worked on farms in my vacations, and at a nearby grain mill with a waterwheel—the owner would give me work when I wanted it, and used to put away a part of my wages for me "just in case," as he would say. I haunted the green and bountiful countryside, but it did not haunt me back. Still, the town grew familiar, wearable, and the vast house enclosed us, although in increasingly separating solitudes, rooms of our own. I can remember those years most easily by the steady progression through school; but we were well aware of the slow edging into war, and then, during the Sunday-morning service, I remember Tom the Beadle suddenly entering the church and painfully climbing the pulpit steps to whisper in my father's ear, and then my father's quiet announcement that war had been declared.

The war disrupted ordinary human time. For anyone over fifty, it forms a huge hinge in time. Nothing, we knew, would be the same again. Our childhood was over at a stroke. The town kept the skeleton of its old life going, but it became the center of a new and shifting one—troops passing through or stationed nearby, local people taking off into uniformed uncertainty, air-raid drills, austerities, school periods given over to cultivating an enormous food garden, my mother becoming attendant medical officer at a recruitment center, my father summoned to serve on a variety of committees, blackouts every evening. From that time on, throughout the war, I cannot put my memory in any presentable order, although I can pull back pieces and happenings in abundance. The impediment to memory, I suspect, is that none of that time was chosen time. In the service, we were moved about the world by decisions so anonymously distant from us that they might have been dice throws; and whatever happened—grotesque, exasperating, ludicrous, horrible as it may have been in its happening—soon receded into impermanence, because forgetting made the war much easier to survive than remembering. It scarcely arises now, either in memory or in dream, for I have instinctively enclosed it in a warp outside real time. It makes no more sense in the memory than it did in its nightmare reality.

The war dispirited my father, and he brooded more; but we were all so occupied then that we never stopped to take stock. The war sent us children in different directions and gave years time to pass. We did not project any future, but after that we met as a family only rarely or accidentally. I felt that my past had been wiped off the blackboard, and that only when the war was over could my chosen life begin. Whithorn, our early Eden, our world without end, our calendar of growing, had vanished forever; and when I went home on leave just before going overseas I realized that our family had changed from a whole into separate parts. The war aged my parents, and when it was over my father moved back to the kindlier west, to a village parish, even smaller than Whithorn but tuned to the seasonal round. When I visited my parents there, separate though we now were, in time, in place, in mind, I saw how close they were, and how the corridor that had preoccupied me with its polarities had been more an illusion of mine than anything else. What I inherited firmly from my father was the way he used time. Knowing what he had to do, he gave his days a shape of his own devising, for he was not bound by any timetable except on Sundays. Sitting at his desk in the evenings, he put his world in order. He owned his own time, and I wanted to do the same somehow. With my mother, I still argued, but we children had always had to bargain for time with her, because she had the kind of restless zeal that fumes at those who do not share it. I found among my father's papers a letter she had written to him when she was in her seventies, from an Edinburgh hospital during a brief stay, a love letter of such tenderness that it made me realize how close they had been, how dependent on each other, across what seemed to us the gulf of their difference.

•

After the war had cooled and subsided and I had separated myself from Scotland, my shifting life began—a long series of transitions. It was too late to return to the garden but not to inhabit temporary gardens. Of the string of houses and countries I inhabited, my memories are clearer—or, at least, clarifiable—since I can recall roughly why I was there, what I was doing, the people who came and went at the time. I still have many friends from those travelling years, and sometimes, scrambling about in the past, a friend and I will come up with something surprising and illuminating to both of us. My son and I, during our travels, spent three years at the end of the sixties living on an old Thames barge converted to a houseboat and moored in a line of others at Chelsea Reach, in London. Not long ago, we sat down and deliberately set about remembering. It was like dredging the Thames, for we recovered a lot of flotsam—sounds and sayings, the sway of the boat rising on the tide, the names and manners of our floating neighbors, incidents, accidents, the cast of characters who crossed our gangplank. We swamped ourselves with memory and returned to the present with a start.

Certain houses, however, retain in my memory a vividness that amounts to haunting—a mill where I once lived in the French Basque country, a street in Barcelona that became a warm locality, a courtyard in Chile that no longer exists, the stony house in the mountains in Spain that served as a retreat for more than twenty years, and that I have absorbed, stone by stone, to the point of being able to assume its silence in my mind. The addresses serve only as starting points: the places are there to wind in, when we have to recall them to clarify the present. But these houses were theatres for such a multiplicity of happenings, of human connections, of moods and modes, that they are mostly touchstones to memory, fixed points for it to start up from, because the houses have, for the most part, outlived our occupation ·f them. What I find my memory doing is reaching back, by way of place, to repeople past time, to recover lost presences, forgotten emotions. I think I remember more vividly through the ear than through the eye. If I can recover a voice, if I can fix the image and sound of someone talking, the atmospherics of place swim back with the sound, and the lost wavelengths reconnect them-

selves, across time, across absence, across loss. Voices remain living, and memory, for once, does not tamper with them. I can
hear at will the measured phrasing of my father's pulpit voice, as
I can the patient encouragement with which he led me through
Tacitus, word by word.

I was with my father for the last month of his life, in a thick
green summer, in the Border village he had come to rest in. Frail
as he was, we would talk in the mornings, and it was to Whithorn
that he always strayed, for it had remained his chosen place, the
time of his life he liked to wander back to. He had once asked me,
a year or two before, to take his ashes there when he died, and I
had promised him solemnly that I would. The box of ashes sat in
my desk drawer in London for over a year before I could make
what is now a complicated journey back to that small, lost place;
but I nodded to the box whenever I opened the drawer, and always felt the pull of memory, the trickle of forgotten details. I
had negotiated for a small plot in the cemetery, and one Christmas
I made the journey north. On a rainy, windswept morning, we
buried the small box, attended by the incumbent minister and a
small knot of aging parishioners, who remembered him and me.
I called on those I still had attachments to, I walked the faint paths
across fields more by instinct than anything else, I made a cursory
visit to the manse. I did not stay long, for, inside, it had assumed
the dimensions of other people—nothing to do with the images
I carried. I did, however, verify that the corridor was not in fact
endless but quite short, and found that the flagstones had given
way to carpet. At twilight, coming back from a circuitous, med-
itative walk, I saw the manse light up suddenly in the early dusk,
and it glowed through so many layers of time for me in that instant that it seemed like a ship that had been moored there forever,
further back than I knew. I did not, however, decide to stay in
Whithorn, although I felt myself no stranger.

There is a certain irresistibility about returning to past places:
the visit may correct the memory or activate it, but it always carries an expectation of surprise. One fall during the sixties, I had

to go unexpectedly to Edinburgh, and, seeing a bus that announced "SELKIRK" as its destination, I climbed aboard it, on a sudden whim, and was soon lumbering south, sparks flying in my memory as the countryside grew at first recognizable and then familiar. As I stepped down into the marketplace, several old films were all rolling at once in my head, and I made my way through a close toward the green back gate, latched on a spring, that I had shouldered open a thousand times. I sprang it open once more, to find not the cavernous house that had been our adolescent battleground, not the towering elm and the monumental beech hedge it had taken me two days to clip into shape, but nothing at all. Open air, bare ground, an idle bulldozer, and a man steadying a theodolite where the yew tree I used to hide myself in had stood. The man told me that within the year a whole housing scheme would take shape where our house once was. I did not go into the past with him. All I found was a surviving sliver of the garden wall, a thin, teetering pillar of stone; but I left without taking even a piece as a touchstone.

> The house that shored my childhood up
> razed to the ground? I stood, amazed,
> gawking at a block of air,
> unremarkable except
> I had hung it once with crazy
> daywish and nightmare.
>
> Expecting to pass a wistful
> indulgent morning, I had sprung the gate.
> Facing me was a wood
> between which and myself
> a whole crow-gabled and slated
> mythology should have stood.
>
> No room now for the rambling
> wry remembering I had planned;
> nor could I replant
> that plot with a second childhood.

Luck, to have been handed
instead a forgettable element,

and not to have had to meet
regretful ghosts in rooms of glass.
That house by now is fairytale
and I can gloss it over
as easily as passing
clear through a wall.

My parents confessed later that they had not been able to bring
themselves to tell any of us about the removal of the house; but
the disquiet, I suspect, lay more with them, although Selkirk was
a place they had never warmed to, never gone back to. In a country like Scotland, where to endure is all, razing an old house
smacks of sacrilege, an insult to the past. Curiously, I was not
particularly disturbed by its absence. Physically, it no longer existed, true, and so could not contradict or confirm by its presence
the mass of memory it had generated. But I felt that if I were to
apply my memory patiently I could rebuild it, restore it, people
it, putting together the enormous jigsaw puzzle of detail to arrive
at the wholeness of a household. But, as Borges reminds us often,
forgetting is not only desirable but necessary; otherwise memory
would overwhelm us. What haunts me most of all, however, is
that the house has not gone, nor have our memories been wiped
clean of it. All I would have to do is find the thread ends and
slowly reel it all in, from dark to light, as when, at the fall of dark,
I would go round the selfsame house from room to room carrying a lighted taper. I would turn on the gas and hold the flame
close to the mantle until it went *Plop!* and lit up, opening my eyes
to a room that no longer exists but is there somewhere, should I
ever want it back.

Basilisks' Eggs

Coming newly into Spanish, I lacked two essentials—a childhood in the language, which I could never acquire, and a sense of its literature, which I could. In my reading progress, from Cervantes to *Mundo Nuevo*, the magazine that launched the present generation of Latin American writers, I had some wise guides—Max Aub, Emir Rodríguez Monegal, Guillermo Cabrera Infante—who pointed me toward whole new territories: the labyrinthine ironies of Borges, the vast, affirming seaways of Neruda. While I was living in London, I read Emir's *Mundo Nuevo*, issue by issue, as it came out, and it was there that I came across the first chapters of Gabriel García Márquez's *One Hundred Years of Solitude*, followed in 1967 by the whole book. I subsequently met and talked at length with García Márquez in Barcelona, and I wrote this piece as a kind of homage to the Latin American writers who brought so much zest and inventiveness to their fictions.

Being an occasional translator, more by accident than by design, I feel somewhat rueful about the whole question of translating between languages. Its mysterious nature can become something of an obsession, for each act of translation is an unprecedented exercise; yet it is an obsession shared by a minority of people who live and read in more than one language, or whose work requires them to function simultaneously on different linguistic planes— spies, displaced persons, the Swiss, international soccer referees, interpreters, travel guides, anthropologists, and explorers. Translators enjoy the status, more or less, of literary mechanics, reassembling texts from one language to function in another; and even if they do more than that, their work is likely to get little more than a passing nod, if it is mentioned at all—understand-ably, for there can be only a very small body of readers capable of passing judgment on translations, and most of us are glad to have them at all. Translators require the self-effacing disposition of saints; and, since a good translation is one in which a work appears to have been written and conceived in the language into which it is translated, good translators grow used to going unre-warded and unnoticed, except by a sharp-nosed troop of donnish reviewers (we call them "the translation police") who seem to spend their reading lives on the lookout for errors.

As far as translations go, the English language is well served. Its great range makes it capable of accommodating Indo-Euro-pean languages quite comfortably, and in recent years our book thirst has given rise to a steady flow of translation, discovering other literatures and giving foreign classics a new lease on life. I remember once checking up in Spain to see which English-lan-guage writers were most translated into Spanish, and being aston-ished to find complete, leather-bound sets of Somerset Maugham and Zane Grey leading the field. The translation barrier is a chancy one, and not everything that crosses it arrives in the best of condition. Vladimir Nabokov once remarked (as few but he are in a position to remark) that while a badly written book is a blunder, a bad translation is a crime. It has occurred to me at times that the translation police might well be given statutory powers to revoke the licenses of unreliable translators, as a service to lan-guage.

It is one thing to read a book in translation; it is quite another to *read* a translation, for that requires two languages, two texts, and an attention hovering between them. Such close reading of translations has something in common with solving word puz-zles, perhaps, but it can prove extraordinarily revealing about the nature of the two languages—about the nature of language itself. Just as knowing more than one language shatters the likelihood of confusing word and thing, so reading the same work in more than one language draws attention to it as a literary construct—gives the work an added dimension, which may or may not enhance it.

It also draws attention to quite another quality of literature—namely, its translatability or untranslatability. Straightforward linear prose can usually pass without much effort into other languages; but there are some works of literature whose verbal complexity appears to doom them to remain in their own language. Lyric poetry, where compression of meaning is most intense, and in which the sound pattern forms part of the total meaning, comes high on the list of untranslatables—Rilke would be a good example—and yet this does not prevent odd felicities of translation at the hands of poets, or even variant translations of the same poem. It is precisely those works that seem by their linguistic intricacy to be untranslatable that often generate real brilliance in a translator. If anyone doubts that pleasure can come from translation, let him look, for instance, at Henri Bué's 1869 version of *Alice in Wonderland* in French, in which even the puns are rendered by equivalent puns, or Barbara Wright's versions of Raymond Queneau, or the Gardner-Levine rendering, with the author's help, of Guillermo Cabrera Infante's *Tres Tristes Tigres*—works in which wordplay apparently indigenous to another language is matched in English. For a translator, untranslatability can be as much a lure as a deterrent.

I keep pinned on my wall a remark made in an interview by Octavio Paz: "Every translation is a metaphor of the poem translated," he says. "In this sense, the phrase 'poetry is untranslatable' is the exact equivalent of the phrase 'all poetry is translatable.' The only possible translation is poetic transmutation, or metaphor. But I would also say that in writing an original poem, we are translating the world, transmuting it. Everything we do is translation, and all translations are in a way creations."

Translation has always been more haphazard than systematic, depending on the enthusiasm of publishers and the dedication of individual translators. André Gide used to maintain that every writer owed it to his own language to translate at least one foreign work to which his talents and temperament were suited, and there is no question that translation has become a more serious and systematic endeavor. The most admirably concerted effort of translation into English in recent years has been the rendering by various hands of the new writing from Latin America—probably the most energetic and inventive body of literature, particularly where the novel is concerned, in present-day writing. Its reputation preceded it into English—a perfect recipe for disappointment—but by now its main works have appeared in English and continue to appear with minimal delay, so that rumor has been given fairly immediate substance, and readers are able to experience it in its impressive diversity. It is a literature with a surprisingly recent momentum. The Uruguayan critic Emir Rodríguez Monegal puts his finger on the year 1940—the year the South American continent became culturally isolated as a result of the Spanish Civil War and, on its heels, the Second World War, and was driven into a preoccupation with its own national identities. From that time on, a reading public has been mushrooming in Latin America, and writers have been virtually summoned into being. It seems a long time since the Great American Novel has even been contemplated in the United States; but Latin-American novelists seem to have their sights set on nothing less. The continent has dawned on them as unwritten history, untapped literary resource—the indigenous Indians, the Spanish Conquest, the stirrings of independence, the subsequent tyrannies, the bizarre immigrations, the economic colonization from Europe and the North, the racial confusions, the paradoxes of national character, the Cuban revolution and military oppressions, the great sprawl and struggle of the present. There exists in Latin America now such enthusiasm about literature that writers are attended to like rock stars. What is more, the writers all read one another, know one another, review one another, and are refreshingly pleased at one another's existence, as though they felt themselves part of a huge literary adventure, a creative rampage. They are enviously placed in time, for part of their literary experience has been to read all the diverse experiments that have taken place in other literatures in the course of this century—experiments of which they have been avid students but not imitators, for their own writing is hugely inventive and varied in its manner.

Just as it would be practically impossible to discover anything like a unified culture in as sprawling a context as Latin America, so is it unfeasible to find or create a common language, for in the hundred and fifty years since the majority of the Latin-American countries gained their independence from Spain the language has been steadily diversifying—separating itself from Castilian Spanish much as American English did from English English, breeding varieties of urban slang, breaking up in many directions—so that writers in search of a new realism seemed doomed instead to an inevitable regionalism. It is to Jorge Luis Borges that Latin-American writers owe one powerful and influential solution to this dilemma, for Borges wrote in a language of his own—a highly literary language, unlike language in currency, a language that draws attention to itself, mocks itself, casts suspicion on itself. From Borges came the beguiling reminder that language is a trick, a manipulation of reality rather than a reflection of it—a notion that stems, after all, from Cervantes. His economy, his playful erudition, his ironies, his treatment of rational knowledge and language as fantastic games dazzled not only Latin Americans but also, in the first translations of his work, a whole crop of American and European writers. He has been both source and challenge, especially to the younger writers, for, although repudiating his archconservatism, they have taken a cue from him in looking for the concomitantly appropriate language for their own fantastic realities.

•

The two writers who have dominated the literary scene in Latin America are Borges and the Chilean poet Pablo Neruda, who died in late 1973. What is most curious about their coexistence is how little they have to do with each other as writers, how seldom they met or even mentioned each other as men, how drastically different their work is, and yet how Latin-American each is, in his separate way. Borges's collected work is as sparse and spare as Neruda's is abundant and ebullient, metaphysical as Neruda's is physical, formal as Neruda's is free-flowing, dubious as Neruda's is passionately affirmative or condemnatory. Where Neruda is open and even naïve, Borges is subtle and skeptical; where Neruda is a sensualist, Borges is an ascetic; where Neruda writes of tangible, physical experience, Borges's fund of experience is purely literary—he looks on reading as a form of time travel. Although Borges roots his stories in Buenos Aires, Latin America is for him something of a metaphor, a geographical fiction. Neruda, quite to the contrary, celebrates, in hymnic joy or rage, the inexhaustible particularity of the Latin-American continent. For him, language is largesse, and his human concern made his political commitment inevitable.

The lives and careers of these two writers have diverged as widely as their work. Borges, suffering from a gradual congenital blindness, lived from his earliest years *within* books and language, fascinated by stories of his soldiering ancestors and of the celebrated knife-fighters of Buenos Aires. What probably distinguishes him most as a writer is the profoundly disquieting effect he has on his readers. However remote and literary his subject matter may appear, he makes the experience of paradox so tangible and eerie that it persists almost as a spell—if after reading Borges one were, say, to miss a train, the event would be dressed in ominous significance. What Borges helped to do for Latin-American writing was to rescue it from the slough of naturalism into which it had fallen and make it once again the province of the individual imagination; but he remains a difficult master in his sheer inimitability. Neruda has proved to be an influence more to the taste of present-day Latin-American writers, if a less directly technical one. His output was prodigious, a progression in which he shed poetic selves like skins, moving from an early wild surrealism in the direction of human engagement and political commitment, never losing his vision but deliberately simplifying his language. It was a lesson in turning literature to account that was not lost on the younger writers, who for the most part see themselves as similarly engaged. Neruda himself, after a long diplomatic career, served as President Salvador Allende's Ambassador to Paris from 1971 until 1973, and died in Chile twelve days after the coup of September 1973—a death that inevitably became symbolic. It is the intensity and scale of his commitment to Latin America that keep him an important figure for the writers who have come after him.

For some years now, I have been translating poems of both Borges and Neruda, coming to know both men well and their work even better, for one never enters the being of a poem as completely as when one is translating it. It is an odd exercise of spirit, to enter another imagination in another language and then to try to make the movement of it happen in English. Untranslatability that no ingenuity can solve does arise, which is to say that some poems *are* untranslatable. (I keep a notebook of these untranslatables, for they are small mysteries, clues to the intricate nature of a language.) To a translator, Borges and Neruda are exigent in different ways. Borges learned English as a child, read voraciously in English, and has been influenced in the formal sense more by English writing—Stevenson, Kipling, Chesterton, Anglo-Saxon poetry, and the English poetic tradition—than by Spanish literature. In his stories, he tends to use English syntactical forms and prose order—making his Spanish curiously stark but easily accessible to English translation. Indeed, translating Borges into English often feels like restoring the work to its natural language, or retranslating it. In his poems, Borges leans heavily on English verse forms and on many of the formal mannerisms of English poetry, so that translating his poems calls for technical ingenuity and prosodic fluency, precision being all-important. His poems are so thoroughly objectified, however, that no great leaps of interpretation have to be made in translating them. It requires only the patience to refine and refine, closer and closer to the original. Neruda's poems present absorbingly different problems, though not just in their extravagance of language, their hugely varying themes and forms; what distinguishes them is their special tone, an intimacy with the physical world, the ability to enter and become things. (Neruda was commonly referred to in the conversation of his friends as *el vate*, the seer.) To translate his poems requires one to enter them and wear them, on the way to finding a similar tone in English. Neruda's larger poems have a vatic intensity that is difficult to contain in credible English, and has its closest affinities with Whitman, an engraving of whom always sat on his writing table. But his more personal lyrics are within closer reach of English, and, given linguistic luck, are not unre-creatable. Translation is a mysterious alchemy in the first place; but it becomes even more so in the experience of entering the language and perception of two writers who have read human experience so differently and have worded it in such distinct ways—of becoming both of them, however temporarily.

It is interesting to compare the fate of these two writers in translation. Borges has earned such attention in English, and the body of his work is so comparatively small, that translating him in his entirety is a feasible project. (This has not been entirely to Borges's advantage, for some of his earlier critical writing, which would have been better left in the decent obscurity it enjoys in Spanish, goes on being dragged into English.) The interest in Borges has one advantage, however, in that his work has been translated by many hands, giving English readers a choice of versions, and a chance to realize what every translator must: that there is no such thing as a definitive translation. Something of the same is true of Neruda's work, and it has benefited particularly from the variety of its translators, since he was so many different poets himself; but, however assiduously he is mined, his work is so vast that only a fraction of it is likely to come satisfactorily into English. He waits, in his fullness, in Spanish. For that reason, I am discouraged from continuing to translate Neruda; but every now and then a poem of his so startles and absorbs me that its equivalence begins to form in English, and I make a version, for the awe of it. Translation becomes an addiction in one special sense: one can always count on it to take one again and again to the threshold of linguistic astonishment.

It is worth noting that both Neruda and Borges put in time as translators. Neruda produced an energetic translation of *Romeo and Juliet* in 1964, and Borges was an early translator of James Joyce, of Virginia Woolf's *Orlando*, and of William Faulkner, the American writer who, with Whitman, has had the most pervasive influence on Latin-American writing. As might be expected, translation has always mesmerized Borges. In an essay on versions of Homer, he has a sentence that is also destined for my wall. "No problem is as consubstantial with the modest mystery of literature," he writes, "as that posed by a translation."

·

"Anything to do with Latin America never sells" used to be a half-humorous maxim in English publishing circles; but with time the opposite has turned out to be true. There was a point in the mid-sixties when publishers began to take that continent very seriously indeed and became literary prospectors, bent on staking their claims. Such avid attention propelled Latin-American writers into a period of prominence that is commonly referred to as *el Boom*, and certainly there seemed more than coincidence to the fact that so many good novelists should be producing such rich work at once, all over the continent. Is there something about the Latin-American experience, apart from its labyrinthine variety and the fact that it is largely unwritten as yet, that makes it exceptionally fertile ground for inventive fiction? The clue lies, possibly, in a phrase used by the Cuban novelist Alejo Carpentier in an introduction, written in Haiti, to his own novel *El Reino de Este Mundo*. I quote the relevant passage:

> [In Haiti] I was discovering, with every step, the marvellous in the real. But it occurred to me furthermore that the ener-

getic presence of the marvellous in the real was not a privilege peculiar to Haiti, but the heritage of all [Latin] America, which, for example, has not finished fixing the inventory of its cosmogonies. The marvellous in the real is there to find at any moment in the lives of the men who engraved dates on the history of the continent, and left behind names which are still celebrated. . . . The fact is that, in the virginity of its landscape, in its coming together, in its ontology, in the Faust, in presence of Indian and Negro, in the sense of revelation arising from its recent discovery, in the fertile mixtures of race which it engendered, [Latin] America is very far from having used up its abundance of mythologies. . . . For what is the story of [Latin] America if not a chronicle of the marvellous in the real?

Lo real maravilloso, the sense of Latin-American reality as an amazement, not only physically but also historically, pervades Carpentier's own novels; and it is an element, an aura, that appears in the work of many Latin-American writers, however else they may differ in preoccupation and vantage point. The compass of Latin-American novels is less that of a total society than of its smaller, more eccentric microcosms—families, villages, tribes, cities, regions. For Latin Americans, theory is the enemy, human eccentricity the norm. *Lo real maravilloso* is a touchstone, not a fiction; and what the Latin-American writers are doing, confidently and inventively, is giving it widely varying individual substance, finding for it the language it demands.

The most remarkable incarnation of *lo real maravilloso* to date—and by now almost the definition of it—is the long novel *Cien Años de Soledad*, or *One Hundred Years of Solitude*, by the Colombian writer Gabriel García Márquez, which was first published in Buenos Aires in 1967 and is still reverberating—at last count, in twenty-odd translated versions. The novel has had a legendary publishing history. García Márquez began to write it in January of 1965, and, as it was in progress, it began to take shape as a rumor. The Mexican novelist Carlos Fuentes published a tantalizing intimation of the book in a Mexican review after reading the first seventy-five pages, and fragments appeared in two or three literary magazines—extraordinary parts of an unimaginable whole. When Editorial Sudamericana published the book, it sold out in days and ran through edition after edition in a continent where native best-sellers hardly ever arise. The book was immediately moved by reviewers beyond criticism into that dimension of essential literary experience occupied by *Alice in Wonderland* and *Don Quixote*. Invoked as a classic, in a year it *became* a classic, and García Márquez, to his discomfort, a literary monument. If it was not the Latin Americans' *Don Quixote*, people said, it would do to go on with. It was everybody's book, for, however intricate a construct it was on the metaphysical level, it was founded on the stark anecdotal flow of Latin-American experience, and everybody who read it discovered a relative or a familiar in it. (García Márquez told me that following the appearance of the German edition he received a letter from a woman in Bavaria threatening legal action on the ground that he had plagiarized her family history.) I saw a copy of the book sticking out of a taxi-driver's glove compartment in Santiago de Chile a few years ago, and he told me he had read it five times; and a group of students I knew in Buenos Aires used to hold an elaborate running quiz on the book, even using it as the basis for a private language, as enthusiasts once did with Joyce's *Ulysses*.

I have already read two or three books, a cluster of essays and reviews, and a profusion of magazine articles on *One Hundred Years of Solitude*; and there must be an uncountable number of theses, both written and to come, unpicking it over and over. It is a difficult book to deal with critically, since it does not yield to categorization or comparison; and there were some bewildered reviews of it, in England and France especially. García Márquez himself, who is the most generous of spirits, declared early on that, having suffered for years as an itinerant newspaperman, he would not deny interviews to his fellows. "I decided that the best way to put an end to the avalanche of useless interviews is to give the greatest number possible, until the whole world gets bored with me and I'm worn out as a subject," he said in one interview; but the world proved tenacious, and printed conversations with him appeared all over the place—some of them whimsical in the extreme, because he doggedly refuses to translate the book into explanation, and is addicted to playing with language and ideas, if not with his interviewers, for he often refers, cryptically and tantalizingly, to the forty-two undiscovered errors in the text.

The criticism that has accrued around *One Hundred Years of Solitude*—and I have read studies on elements as diverse as the biblical references in the text and the topography of the province of Magdalena, in Colombia, in which both the book and García Márquez are rooted—is the best testimony to his inexhaustibility, and is compulsive reading, in that a classic is a book that one cannot know too much about, a book that deepens with each reading.

The Peruvian writer Mario Vargas Llosa published, in 1971, a six-hundred-and-sixty-seven-page vade mecum entitled *García Márquez: Historia de un Deicidio* (García Márquez: The Story of a Godkiller), a biographical and critical study that painstakingly elucidates the writer's background and influences, his four early books and stories, his preoccupations (or *demonios*, as Vargas Llosa calls them), his literary ancestors, and the writing of *One Hundred Years of Solitude*. Vargas Llosa's book is unlikely to be translated into English, and that is a pity, for it is a most absorbing chronicle of a book's coming into being, of a long and complex creative unwinding. His main claim for the novel is worth quoting in full:

> *One Hundred Years of Solitude* is a *total* novel, in the direct line of those dimensionally ambitious creations that compete with reality on an equal footing, confronting it with the image of a qualitatively equivalent vastness, vitality, and complexity. This totality shows itself first in the plural nature of the novel, in its being apparently contradictory things at once: traditional and modern, local and universal, imaginative and realistic. Another expression of its totality is its limitless accessibility, its quality of being within reach, with distinct but abundant rewards for each one, for the intelligent

reader and the imbecile, for the serious person who savors the prose, admires the architecture, and unravels the symbols in a work of fiction, and for the impatient reader who is only after crude anecdote. The literary spirit of our time is most commonly hermetic, oppressed, and minority-centered. *One Hundred Years of Solitude* is one of those rare instances, a major contemporary work of literature that everyone can understand and enjoy.

But *One Hundred Years of Solitude* is a total novel above all because it puts into practice the utopian design of every God-supplanter: to bring into being a complete reality, confronting actual reality with an image that is its expression and negation. Not only does this notion of totality, so slippery and complex, but so inseparable from the vocation of novelist, define the greatness of *One Hundred Years of Solitude*; it gives the clue to it. *One Hundred Years of Solitude* qualifies as a total novel both in its subject matter, to the extent that it describes an enclosed world, from its birth to its death, and all the orders that make it up—individual and collective, legendary and historical, day-to-day and mythical—and in its form, inasmuch as the writing and the structure have, like the material that takes shape in them, an exclusive, unrepeatable, and self-sufficient nature.

One Hundred Years of Solitude, as everyone must know by now, tells the story of the founding of the town of Macondo by José Arcadio Buendía and his wife, Úrsula Iguarán, and of the vagaries of the Buendía family through six generations of plagues, civil war, economic invasion, prosperity, and decline, up to the impending death of the last surviving Buendía and the disintegration of Macondo. The presiding spirit of the Buendía family is the old gypsy magus Melquíades, who, finding the solitude of death unbearable, returns to instruct those members of the family able to see him, and whose coded parchments, deciphered, ultimately, by the last Buendía, prove to be the book we are reading, since Melquíades is able to see backward and forward in time, as the novelist is. Melquíades's parchments "had concentrated a century of daily episodes in such a way that they coexisted in one instant," just as García Márquez has done. Throughout the torrential progress of the book, time is both foreseen and remembered, its natural sequence disrupted by premonition and recurrence. Magical happenings, supernatural perceptions, miracles, and cataclysmic disasters are so closely attendant on characters and events that the book seems to contain all human history compressed into the vicissitudes of a village, and yet each of the Buendías is eccentrically and memorably separate as a character. García Márquez is bewitched by the notion of fiction as a form of magic, which can make free with human time. For the novelist, "everything is known," as Melquíades reiterates in the book. And toward the end of the novel García Márquez observes, in the persona of Aureliano Buendía, that "literature was the best toy ever invented for making fun of people"—a conviction that would certainly be shared by an antic Borges.

The same preoccupation with literature as a secret language is apparent in the fact that García Márquez has strewn the text with personal allusions—dates correspond to the birthdays of his family and friends, his wife appears fleetingly as a character, as he does himself, family jokes are written in—adding to the book a private dimension of his own. In the same way, the book invokes the works of his fellow Latin-American novelists. The names of characters from novels of Carlos Fuentes, Julio Cortázar, and Alejo Carpentier crop up in the text, a passage recalls Juan Rulfo, and there are scenes consciously in the manner of Carpentier, Asturias, and Vargas Llosa, in a kind of affectionate homage. "Every good novel is a riddle of the world," García Márquez remarked to Vargas Llosa; and the more one discovers about the book and its genesis—thanks largely to Vargas Llosa—the more one realizes that García Márquez emptied himself into it totally. It is the coming into being of the book, in fact, that turns out to be the most revealing clue to its extraordinary nature.

To Vargas Llosa, García Márquez made a statement that would appear to be another of his whimsies except for the fact that he has emphasized the point many times. "Everything I have written I knew or I had heard before I was eight years old," he said.

"From that time on, nothing interesting has happened to me."
Talking to the critic Plinio Apuleyo Mendoza, he also said, "In
my books, there is not a single line that is not founded on a real
happening. My family and my old friends are well aware of it.
People say to me, 'Things just happen to you that happen to no
one else.' I think they happen to everybody, but people don't have
the sensibility to take them in or the disposition to notice them."
One Hundred Years of Solitude is so full of improbable happenings
and apparently grotesque invention that it seems at first perverse
of García Márquez to claim these as part of his boyhood experience. Yet I think that these statements have to be taken very seriously indeed, for, on examination, they throw a great deal of light
on the genesis and nature of the novel.

•

García Márquez was born in 1928 in the township of Aracataca,
in the Colombian province of Magdalena, in the swampy region
between the Caribbean and the mountains, and for the first eight
years of his life—the crucial years, by his own account—his parents left him behind in Aracataca, in the care of his maternal
grandparents, Colonel Nicolás Márquez Iguarán and Doña Tranquilina Iguarán Cotes. His grandparents had settled in Aracataca
when it was little more than a village, in the wake of the pulver-
izing civil war, the War of a Thousand Days, which lasted from
1899 until 1903, and in which Colonel Márquez had fought on
the Liberal side against the Conservatives, Aracataca itself being
a Liberal outpost. They had lived there through the frenzied years
of the "green gold"—the banana fever that brought foreign ex-
ploiters and relative prosperity to the region and then subsided
around 1920 in a wave of disaffection and economic distress. The
grandparents were first cousins, and enjoyed a position of esteem
in Aracataca, occupying the most prominent house in the place—
a house that they peopled with stories. It was through his grandparents that the bulk of the material that later gushed out in *One
Hundred Years of Solitude* entered García Márquez's awareness;
they remain, he says, the dominant influence in his life, in their

separate ways. Vargas Llosa's account of the novelist's childhood draws attention to circumstances and events in these early years that later found their place in the novel. One of García Márquez's earliest memories is of his grandfather's leading him by the hand through the town to see a travelling circus—a foreshadowing of the first chapter of the novel. The Colonel would read to the boy from the encyclopedia and from *The Thousand and One Nights*, the only books he remembers from these years, and would ply him with stories of the civil war, in which the Colonel had been a companion-in-arms of the Liberal General Rafael Uribe Uribe, whose exploits became the model for Colonel Aureliano Buendía in the novel. To read the history of the War of a Thousand Days is bizarre enough; but to have it recounted and embellished by an old man who took part in it, and who must in any case have assumed mythic proportions for the boy, must have lodged all that material deep enough for it to go undented by fact or subsequent experience. Tales of the banana fever, which brought Aracataca a sudden prosperity and a foreign population, reached him in the same way—from the people who had lived through it. His grandfather waited throughout his life for a chimerical pension promised to Liberal veterans by the Conservatives but never delivered—a state of affairs that is the spine of García Márquez's earlier and most celebrated story, "No One Writes to the Colonel," a noble invocation of the spirit of his grandfather. There are other precise precedents: as a young man, Colonel Márquez had been forced to kill a man in a dispute and, although in the right, had had to settle in a new town—the same circumstance that leads to the founding of Macondo by José Arcadio Buendía. García Márquez remembers his grandfather's saying to him repeatedly, "You cannot imagine how much a dead man weighs." Colonel Márquez also fathered a crop of illegitimate sons during the civil wars, as does Colonel Aureliano Buendía in the novel. Already, the two worlds are difficult to keep separate. People, events past and present, real and fabulous, the encyclopedia and *The Thousand and One Nights*—all occupy the same dimension.

García Márquez has always claimed that his literary style came from his grandmother, Doña Tranquilina; and she is certainly the source of the novel's extraordinary women, whose domestic intuitions challenge the excessive and often misguided rationality of the men. He recalls her waking him up in bed to tell him stories; and she would keep up a running conversation in the large, empty house with dead relatives, so that to him the house seemed peopled with presences. She appears to have drawn no distinction between legend and event, nor would any such distinction have made much sense to García Márquez at that time. It is to her that he attributes the blurring of the magical with the real. In an interview with Plinio Apuleyo Mendoza, he cites one example:

> When I was about five, an electrician came to our house to change the meter. He came a number of times. On one of them, I found my grandmother trying to shoo a yellow butterfly from the kitchen with a cloth and muttering, "Every time that man comes, this yellow butterfly appears in the house."

The memory is transmogrified in the novel into the character of Mauricio Babilonia, whose appearances are always accompanied by yellow butterflies. Another of the magical happenings in the novel—when Remedios the Beauty, an unearthly creature beyond human love, whose appearance drives men wild, ascends one day into Heaven as she is folding sheets in the garden—is clarified by García Márquez in conversation with Vargas Llosa:

> The explanation of that is much simpler, much more banal than it appears. There was a girl who corresponded exactly to my description of Remedios in the book. Actually, she ran away from home with a man, and the family, not wishing to face the shame of it, announced, straight-faced, that they had seen her folding sheets in the garden and that afterward she had ascended into Heaven. At the moment of writing, I preferred the family's version to the real one.

Similarly, the strike of banana workers in the novel, which ends in their being massacred, is based on the killing of striking banana workers in Ciénaga, in the province of Magdalena, in 1928. García Márquez remembers hearing stories of it as a boy, but at the same time hearing it denied by others, who accepted the official lie, that it had never happened, just as the survivors in Macondo are made to disremember it. As a boy, listening to the running fables of Aracataca, he drew no line between the fabulous and the real, the true and the false, the subjective and the objective. With the stories, a world entered whole into his imagination. The problem when he faced the writing of *One Hundred Years of Solitude* was to find a way of reproducing that wholeness.

Without further example, I think we can take García Márquez with complete seriousness when he talks of the superimportance of those first eight years. They also throw light on the "solitude" of the title, which is the solitude he describes himself as experiencing in the vast house in Aracataca, with its ghosts and its stories, temporarily abandoned by his own parents to the care of the two eccentric grandparents, whose lives seemed so remote from his own. All the Buendías in the book are similarly enclosed in the glass bubbles of their own destinies, fulfilling separate fates, touching one another only briefly, in passing, possessed by their own secrets.

Given that his early life was a tangible experiencing of *lo real maravilloso*, this was far from a guarantee that García Márquez was to become a writer; if that were so, we should be knee-deep in extraordinary novels. More had to happen; and perhaps the decisive experience was a journey García Márquez took with his mother back to Aracataca to sell the house of his grandparents some seven years after he had left it, on their death. He describes the shock of discovering the town, and the house of his childhood, transposed by time, shrunken, empty, altered. The experience, he says, imprinted deeply in him the desire to find and preserve the Aracataca of his grandparents, the wholeness of his first world; he could not credit that it no longer existed. It did exist; or, at least, it would. On that same journey, Aracataca was metamorphosed into Macondo, the mythical Aracataca of his boyhood; for as the train came to a halt close to the town he saw out of its window the name Macondo on a sign. Macondo was the name of a run-down banana plantation; but it also had a certain currency in local legend as a kind of never-never land from which people did not return.

From that point on, García Márquez lived an itinerant life that produced four books, stories, film scripts, and a slew of newspaper articles. He began, very young, a book—which he never finished—called *La Casa*, an evocation of the legendary house of his grandparents. He threw himself into a literary apprenticeship, reading Amadís de Gaul, Defoe, Rabelais, Balzac, Hemingway, Faulkner, Virginia Woolf, Camus—all the authors who have been invoked as influences on his work. But he was after something in which they could only assist him. He became a journalist, first in Colombia, then in Europe and the United States, turning his attention to writing on his own when he could; but these were turbulent years for him, and the book inside him seemed perpetually out of reach. It was not until he was settled in Mexico in the sixties, writing film scripts after a period of barrenness, that he suddenly found what he had been seeking so long—the focus and the manner ample enough to contain the wholeness of his early vision. He describes to Vargas Llosa how, one day in January of 1965, he was driving his family from Mexico City to Acapulco when the book tugged imperatively at his sleeve. "It was so clear that I could have dictated the first chapter there and then, word for word." He turned the car, went back to Mexico City, closeted himself for the next eighteen months, working every day without letup, and emerged at the end with the complete manuscript of *One Hundred Years of Solitude*, which was immediately accepted by Editorial Sudamericana, in Buenos Aires, and was published, in June of 1967, with almost no emendations.

The four books García Márquez wrote on the way to *One Hundred Years of Solitude*—the novel *La Hojarasca* (Leaf Storm), published in 1955; the long story "El Coronel No Tiene Quien Le Escriba" ("No One Writes to the Colonel"), published in 1958; the novel *La Mala Hora* (The Evil Hour), of 1961; and the collection of stories *Los Funerales de la Mamá Grande* (Big Mama's Funeral), of 1962—are now, inevitably, combed by readers for any signs of and references to the huge flowering that followed; and, indeed, *Leaf Storm* is set in Macondo, which also makes a more substantial appearance in *Big Mama's Funeral*. It is easy to understand the frustration García Márquez felt on the publication of each book, for he had not yet found a way of writing adequate to contain and keep whole the intricate vision he had of his own many-layered Macondo. But the early books show him to be a considerable story writer; "No One Writes to the Colonel" is a meticulously well-written, spare story, its character beautifully drawn. The early stories are understated and ironic, but by the time García Márquez came to write the story "Big Mama's Funeral" the surface realism had begun to crack, and excursions of fancy intruded into the narrative. In the novels, too, he was experimenting—in *Leaf Storm* with writing of the same reality from different vantage points, and in *The Evil Hour* with the complexities of a text within a text. But a spare realism could not contain the bulging of the imagination that was showing up increasingly in his work.

Two things were still lacking to the novelist—a unifying tone and manner to contain the immense running narrative, and some device to allow him the all-seeing vantage point he required as narrator. It is worth taking another look at where García Márquez stood in relation to the material, the unwritten book, at this stage. He had clear and detailed in his head the magical Macondo narrated to him whole by his grandparents, and the boy's perception of it in its wholeness, and he had the memory of going back later and perceiving its disintegration, its death. This double perception made him into a magical being, a child with foreknowledge. The novelist also has foreknowledge. But what must have eluded García Márquez all this time was where and how to situate himself in relation to his narrative.

The solution, clearly, must have come to him in the form of Melquíades, the old gypsy magus, who is befriended by José Arcadio Buendía, the founder of Macondo, and who occasionally returns from death to attend certain of the Buendías. Melquíades knows past and future. He records the whole history of the Buendía family in code on his parchments, but they are condemned to live in time, and cannot know it. So as Melquíades the novelist could situate himself in the proper magical relation to his narrative, since for him, too, everything is known. Melquíades's parchments are to be the novel.

The first sentence of the novel shows just what use García Márquez makes of his magical persona: "Many years later, as he faced the firing squad, Colonel Aureliano Buendía was to remember that distant afternoon when his father took him to discover ice." In it we are projected forward from the present to a vantage point in the future from which we look backward at what is taking place. We are situated in both dimensions at once. Thus the story is told, looking backward, of a present full of premonition; and memory and dream and fable and miracle are able to intrude into the narrative without any inconsistency. The novel as story is freed from linear time, and sentences are able to refer backward and forward, although firmly rooted in the physicality of the present. "When the pirate Sir Francis Drake attacked Riohacha in the sixteenth century, Úrsula Iguarán's great-great-grandmother became so frightened with the ringing of alarm bells and the firing of cannons that she lost control of her nerves and sat down on a lighted stove." The accident causes her family to move to a settlement where they befriend the Buendía family, and is repeatedly invoked as the initiatory event in the eventual history of Macondo, for Úrsula eventually marries José Arcadio Buendía and, as a consequence, "every time that Úrsula became exercised over her husband's mad ideas, she would leap back over three hundred years of fate and curse the day that Sir Francis Drake had attacked Riohacha." The remote past crops up in the running present; the generations of the Buendías reflect one another, forward and backward. And as Aureliano Babilonia, the last surviving Buendía, is given by his imminent death the insight to decode the parchments of Melquíades, he discovers "that Sir Francis Drake had attacked Riohacha only so that they could seek each other through the most intricate labyrinths of blood until they would engender the mythological animal that was to bring the line to an end." The narrative continues: "It was foreseen that the city of mirrors (or mirages) would be wiped out by the wind and exiled from the memory of men at the precise moment when Aureliano Babilonia would finish deciphering the parchments, and that everything written on them was unrepeatable since time immemorial and forever more, because races condemned to one hundred years of solitude did not have a second opportunity on earth."

•

In a long published interview with Fernández Brasó, García Márquez spoke of his search for a style:

> I had to live twenty years and write four books of apprenticeship to discover that the solution lay at the very root of the problem: I had to tell the story, simply, as my grandparents told it, in an imperturbable tone, with a serenity in the face of evidence which did not change even though the world were falling in on them, and without doubting at any moment what I was telling, even the most frivolous or the most truculent, as though these old people had realized that in literature there is nothing more convincing than conviction itself.

It is the word "imperturbable" that leaps out; it is the key to the running tone of *One Hundred Years of Solitude*. Surprising events are chronicled without any expression of surprise, and comic events with a straight face; the real and the magical are juxtaposed without comment or judgment; the dead and living interact in the same unaltering prose dimension. García Márquez is an accomplished exaggerator, as was his grandfather, by repute; but his Neruda-like lists of wonders have a numerical exactness which humanizes them and makes them into facts of perception. The rains that devastate Macondo last "for four years, eleven months, and two days." The astonishing is made matter-of-fact, and the matter-of-fact is a running astonishment: "Colonel Aureliano Buendía organized thirty-two armed uprisings and he lost them all. He had seventeen male children by seventeen different women and they were exterminated one after the other on a single night before the oldest one had reached the age of thirty-five. He survived fourteen attempts on his life, seventy-three ambushes, and a firing squad." The spinster Amaranta Buendía has a clear and unperturbed premonition of her own death:

> She saw it because it was a woman dressed in blue with long hair, with a sort of antiquated look, and with a certain resemblance to Pilar Ternera during the time when she had helped with the chores in the kitchen. . . . Death did not tell her when she was going to die . . . but ordered her to begin sewing her own shroud on the next sixth of April. She was authorized to make it as complicated and as fine as she wanted . . . and she was told that she would die without pain, fear, or bitterness at dusk on the day that she finished it. Trying to waste the most time possible, Amaranta ordered some rough flax and spun the thread herself. She did it so carefully that the work alone took four years. Then she started the sewing. . . . One week before she calculated that she would take the last stitch on the night of February 4, and, without revealing the motives, she suggested to Meme that she move up a clavichord concert that she had arranged for the day after. . . . At eight in the morning, she took the last stitch in the most beautiful piece of work that any woman had ever finished, and she announced without the least bit of dramatics that she was going to die at dusk. She not only told the family but the whole town, because Amaranta had conceived of the idea that she could make up for a

life of meanness with one last favor to the world, and she thought that no one was in a better position to take letters to the dead.

The book is rooted in the domestic detail of the Buendía household; tragedy, disaster, and death are accommodated, along with magical events, as they intrude into the continuing life of the family. One of the Buendía sons is shot in another part of Macondo:

A trickle of blood came out under the door, crossed the living room, went out into the street, continued on in a straight line across the uneven terraces, went down steps and climbed over curbs, passed along the Street of the Turks, turned a corner to the right and another to the left, made a right angle at the Buendía house, went in under the closed door, crossed through the parlor, hugging the walls so as not to stain the rugs, went on to the other living room, made a wide curve to avoid the dining-room table, went along the porch with the begonias, and passed without being seen under Amaranta's chair as she gave an arithmetic lesson to Aureliano José, and went through the pantry and came out in the kitchen, where Úrsula was getting ready to crack thirty-six eggs to make bread.

In addition to maintaining its even, unsurprised tone, the narrative is reduced starkly to its physical essentials; the astonishment is left to the reader. The novel is crowded with events and characters, comic, grotesque, real and unreal (the distinction no longer has meaning), and the transitions are bland and direct. The touchstone is the running narrative of the writer's grandparents, as perceived by the innocent, unjudging, undifferentiating eye of the boy in Aracataca. When movies are first shown in Macondo, the townspeople "became indignant over the living images that the prosperous merchant Bruno Crespi projected in the theatre with the lion-head ticket windows, for a character who had died and was buried in one film and for whose misfortune tears of affliction had been shed would reappear alive and transformed into an Arab in the next one," and "the audience, who paid two cents apiece to share the difficulties of the actors, would not tolerate that outlandish fraud and they broke up the seats." In Macondo, the wheel is invented with daily regularity.

But the ruthless paring down to physical essentials and the even, matter-of-fact tone are not the only distinguishing features of the book's style; its other remarkable element is its rhythm, its flow. The sentences are constructed with a running inevitability to them. The narrative never pauses but flows on, impervious to the events, disastrous and wondrous, it relates; it is time flowing, the steady current of day-to-day detail. In that flow everything is synthesized and swept along, everything is contained. It is the rhythm that lends the book its feeling of process. Nothing stops the flow of the narrative. Conversations are gnomic exchanges in passing. The book flows on like running water to its inevitable end, which leaves us holding the deciphered version of Melquíades's parchments, ready to begin them again.

Things go round again in the same cycles; progress is an illusion, change merely an attribute of time—these attitudes implicit in the book exude from the history and being not just of Aracataca-Macondo and Colombia but of the Latin-American continent. Yet the manner in which this fate is accepted and come to terms with is what gives Latin Americans their distinguishing humanity; their measure is a human one. The solitude of the Buendías is their fate; but their reactions to that fate are supremely human—obsessively Promethean and absurdly courageous on the part of the men, tenacious and down-to-earth on the part of the women—and are always leavened with a humorous energy. They assume to the full the responsibility of being their idiosyncratic selves. For the inhabitants of Macondo, there is no body of outside knowledge to refer to. What they know is what they perceive; what they come to terms with is their fate, their own death. García Márquez's twin obsessions—with the original, eccentric sense of human awe lodged in him as a child, and with the discovery of a language ample enough to contain that view in its wholeness—come together so inextricably in *One Hundred Years of Solitude* that the world becomes a book.

The degree to which *One Hundred Years of Solitude* has been acclaimed in translation is a measure of how successful García Márquez is in universalizing his material. Almost monotonously, the book has been named best foreign novel as it has emerged in other languages. The Italians and the Yugoslavs turned apoplectic in their praise of it, while English reviewers almost universally referred to it as "a fantasy"—a term one must be extremely cautious about applying to García Márquez. Obviously, the book was not being lost in translation; but then for a translator it raises no insurmountable technical problems. The language is crystal-clear and physical, the wordplay is minimal, the vocabulary exotic but containable. The challenge for a translator lies in reproducing the extraordinary running rhythm of the original—García Márquez's sentences are carefully phrased, musically, for the ear; the narrative movement is orchestrated by their rhythm, as García Márquez's own recorded reading of the first chapter makes particularly clear. I can only wonder whether the rhythm of the original is possible to maintain in languages with a sound pattern drastically different from Spanish. But where the rhythm is concerned the English translation, by Gregory Rabassa, is something of a masterpiece, for it is almost matched to the tune of the Spanish, never lengthening or shortening sentences but following them measure for measure. García Márquez insists that he prefers the English translation to the original, which is tantamount to saying they are interchangeable—the near-unattainable point of arrival for any translator.

•

The enthusiastic attention universally attracted by *One Hundred Years of Solitude* propelled García Márquez into a limelight he had not reckoned on, and for a time he became the running prey of literary interviewers and inquisitors, and the center of international curiosity. The question that preoccupied readers most—as it must have preoccupied him—was, What could he write next? *One Hundred Years of Solitude* had freed him from the obsessive preoccupation with unloading into language the Aracataca of his grandparents as he had perceived it; yet it had put a strain of expectation on his work. In 1972, he published a collection of seven new stories, under the title *La Increíble y Triste Historia de la Cándida Eréndira y de su Abuela Desalmada* (The Incredible and Sad Tale of Innocent Eréndira and Her Heartless Grandmother). The title story had had two previous existences—one as a long anecdote in *One Hundred Years of Solitude*, and the other as a film script—and now it arrived in a longer and more exotic version, like a written circus. Eréndira burns down her grandmother's house by accident, and she, in revenge, prostitutes her granddaughter in carnival procession through the villages of an interminable desert landscape to recoup her losses. The bare bones of the anecdote are fleshed out in the story, however, with an exuberance of detail and a mythic extension that clearly carry over from the novel; and in the other stories the realistic surface of things has all but disappeared. "The Sea of Lost Time," "A Very Old Man with Enormous Wings," "The Handsomest Drowned Man in the World," "Blacamán the Good, Vendor of Miracles," "The Last Voyage of the Ghost Ship": the titles alone give some indication of where we are—face to face with magical events and extraordinary figures that, although they are no longer in Macondo, belong to the same dimension and wavelength, in which wonders are natural happenings. Most conspicuously, the style continues in the vein of exotic enumeration, imperturbably precise in the face of wonders.

One of the stories, "The Last Voyage of the Ghost Ship," is written in a manner that attempts to bring all its elements into a fusion even tighter than in the novel. Once a year a boy in a seaside village has the vision of a huge liner without lights sailing across the bay in front of the village. He is disbelieved, first by his mother and then, on a subsequent occasion, by the villagers, who beat and ridicule him, so the following year he lies in wait, in a stolen rowboat, and leads the liner aground on the shoal in front of the village church. The story, dense in physical detail, is a running narrative of six pages, a single sentence that encompasses past and dream as part of a flowing present, a stream of consciousness not confined to any one consciousness—for characters intrude in the first person, the focal point keeps shifting, the objective and the subjective are parts of a larger whole. Again, the images are threaded on the continuing string of the rhythm. It was clear from this story that García Márquez had not yet satisfied his linguistic curiosity.

Extravagant of imagination, these stories showed him more determined than ever to embrace the wondrous as part of the natural—to destroy the distinction, to insist on the marvellous as real. He also seemed to be trying to embed linear narrative episodically in a larger language; but he could not abandon it, for he is an instinctive storyteller, most probably because of his profound experience as a listener. The compulsion intrudes into his conversation; he enfables his day. On one occasion, in Barcelona, when we met after an interim, I noticed that he had given up smoking—surprisingly, for he had been a fierce smoker. "I will tell you how to be free of smoking," he said to me. "First, you must decide that the cigarette, a dear friend who has been close to you for many years, is about to die. Death, as we know, is irremediable. You take a pristine packet of your favorite cigarettes—mine were those short black Celtas—and you bury it, with proper ceremony, in a grave you have prepared in the garden—I made a headstone for mine. Then, every Sunday—not oftener, for the memory is painful—you put flowers on the grave, and give thanks. Time passes. For me now, the cigarette is dead, and I have given up mourning."

In occasional interviews, García Márquez spoke of the book he was writing: a phantasmagorical study of a dictator who has lived for two hundred years; an exploration of the solitude of power. The book was a long time in the writing, and was promised long before it arrived, but was eventually published in March of 1975 under the title of *El Otoño del Patriarca*. The first Spanish reviews were tinged with disappointment, since the reviewers obviously wanted to be back in Macondo. It took time for the book to separate itself from the powerful shadow of *One Hundred Years of Solitude*. Besides, it is a book requiring very attentive reading at first, until one grows more comfortably familiar with its extraordinary style, for it goes even further, along the lines of "The Last Voyage of the Ghost Ship," toward fusing all its sprawling elements into one single stream of prose.

The book is set in an unspecified Caribbean country which is under the sway of a dictator who has lived longer than anyone can remember; and it is no more specific of time and place than that. Its point of departure— and the starting point for each of its six chapters—is a mob breaking into the decaying palace to find the dictator dead. As they poke wonderingly among the ruins of the palace, with "the felt on the billiard tables cropped by cows," they begin to brood, in their collective consciousness, on incidents in the dictator's reign, and the narrative shifts to these events, then passes without pausing into the dictator's consciousness, back into events and other consciousnesses, in continuous change. Linear time is abandoned, and even deliberately confused; everyone has forgotten the sequence of events while vividly remembering and juxtaposing the events themselves. Each chapter encompasses two or three crucial episodes in the dictator's career—set pieces of the imagination, like separate García Márquez stories inserted in the flow—alongside the natural and unnatural disasters: the occasional massacres of plotting generals, the coming of a comet, the occupation of the country by marines of a foreign power, the eventual selling of the country's sea. The dictator himself is never named, and there are only a few fully rounded, fully identified characters: the dictator's mother, Benedición Alvarado, the simple woman who accompanies him anxiously into power, and in whose memory, when his attempts to canonize her have failed, he declares war against the Holy See; his crony General Rodrigo de Aguilar, who, when he is discovered to be a traitor, is served up by the dictator, roasted and garnished, at a feast of his brother officers; the novice nun Leticia Nazareno, whom he impulsively marries and is dominated by, and who, with her young son, already a general, is torn to pieces by specially trained wild dogs; Manuela Sánchez, the gypsy queen, who beguiles the dictator into transforming suburbs for her pleasure; José Ignacio Saenz de la Barra, his sleek and sinister favorite, who initiates a reign of terror the dictator can only survive, not control. The narrative keeps being picked up by other voices, other consciousnesses, always sharp in physical detail. There is a pervading domesticity to García Márquez's frame of reference; in one long passage we follow the dictator through the long and finicky ritual of going to bed, in the course of which he patrols the palace, dressing objects in asides of memory.

Technically, what García Márquez does in *The Autumn of the Patriarch* is to dispense with the sentence altogether as the unit of his prose, and substitute an intelligible flow that encompasses several shifts in vantage point. In one passage, the dictator is being besieged in his palace:

> I already told you not to pay them any heed, he said, dragging his graveyard feet along the corridors of ashes and scraps of carpets and singed tapestries, but they're going to keep it up, they told him, they had sent word that the flaming balls were just a warning, that the explosions will come after general sir, but he crossed the garden without paying attention to anyone, in the last shadows he breathed in the sound of the newborn roses, the disorders of the cocks in the sea wind, what shall we do general, I already told you not to pay

any attention to them, God damn it, and as on every day at that hour he went to oversee the milking, so as on every day at that hour the insurrectionists in the Conde barracks saw the mule cart with the six barrels of milk from the presidential stable appear, and in the driver's seat there was the same lifetime carter with the oral message that the general sends you this milk even though you keep on spitting in the hand that feeds you, he shouted it out with such innocence that General Bonivento Barboza gave the order to accept it on the condition that the carter taste it first so that they could be sure it wasn't poisoned, and then they opened the iron gates and the fifteen hundred rebels looking down from the inside balconies saw the cart drive in to center on the paved courtyard, they saw the orderly climb up onto the driver's seat with a pitcher and a ladle to give the carter the milk to taste, they saw him uncork the first barrel, they saw him floating in the ephemeral backwash of a dazzling explosion and they saw nothing else to the end of time in the volcanic heat of the mournful yellow mortar building in which no flower ever grew, whose ruins remained suspended for an instant in the air from the tremendous explosion of the six barrels of dynamite.

What García Márquez is after is a language that can contain individual consciousnesses but is not confined by any one, a language that can encompass a whole human condition, that can accommodate the contradictory illusions of which it is made up. Objective truth is only one illusion among a number of illusions, individual and tribal. Consciousness can be neither linear nor serial. The text, though still as sharp in physical particulars as ever, raises infinitely more problems for the translator than its predecessor did, for its sudden shifts in focus have to be handled in language in such a way as to take the reader's attention with them. Rabassa manages these beautifully. Again, his version is more than a translation: it is a matching in English of the original.

The book's preoccupation is with appearance, deception, and illusion, with lies transformed into illusions by the power of belief. Behind illusion there is only solitude—in this case, the solitude of power. The dictator, who can neither read nor write, governs "orally and physically." His power is beyond reason:

> you find him alive and bring him to me and if you find him
> dead bring him to me alive and if you don't find him bring
> him to me, an order so unmistakable and fearsome that be
> fore the time was up they came to him with the news general
> sir that they had found him.

The only person ever to tell him the truth is his double, Patricio Aragonés, as he is dying of poison meant for the dictator, but the dictator knows that truth is only his own whim, and language only another deception. Tuned in to the betrayals of others, he survives long beyond the point where his power has any meaning, a shambling old man-child trying to get a night's rest for his accompanying infirmities from his own grotesque and imperturbable image. Close to death (his second death, since he used the death of his double in order to claim rebirth), he broods:

> he learned to live with those and all the miseries of glory as
> he discovered in the course of his uncountable years that a
> lie is more comfortable than doubt, more useful than love,
> more lasting than truth, he had arrived without surprise at
> the ignominious fiction of commanding without power, of
> being exalted without glory and of being obeyed without
> authority.

The illusion of his power is, however, sustained by everyone around him, so that he has no choice but to wear it. He keeps alive by his acute cunning, his nose for deception; at one point (after he has been taught to read by Leticia Nazareno), "the final oracles that governed his fate were the anonymous graffiti on the walls of the servants' toilets, in which he would decipher the hidden truths that no one would have dared reveal to him, not even you, Leticia, he would read them at dawn on his way back from the milking. . . . broadsides of hidden rancor which matured in the warm impunity of the toilets and ended up coming out onto the streets." Fictions outlive the need for them but refuse to die. The only refuge from deceptions is in solitude, yet it is out of solitude that we create the fictions to sustain us.

In *The Autumn of the Patriarch* García Márquez moves toward a complete mythifying of experience, into a total flow that cannot be checked by any reality. Realities of Colombian history occur as fact, legend, and lie, all three; rumor, gossip, fairy tale, dream, illusion, memory all tumble over one another in the book's perception. It has to be taken whole, for wholeness, again, is what it is after. The grossness of its cruelties and lecheries is told in an even, unwavering tone, grotesque in detail; they are part of the book's condition. García Márquez is more concerned with dictatorship as myth in the popular mind (that fountain of invention to which he appears to have unlimited access). Like *One Hundred Years of Solitude*, the book ought to be given three or four readings, for it deserves them, and rewards them. It is a formidable piece of invention, and it pushes the discoveries of *One Hundred Years of Solitude* further, closer to a contained whole. García Márquez's writing has always been illuminated by the transformations his imagination is capable of making, the humanity of his perception, his accurate astonishment, even on the small scale, in a phrase or a minor incident. Patricio Aragonés upbraids the dictator for "making me drink turpentine so I would forget how to read and write." The dictator, waking up suddenly in fear, "felt that the ship of the universe had reached some port while he was asleep." And, we are told, "on one national holiday she [the dictator's mother] had made her way through the guard of honor with a basket of empty bottles and reached the presidential limousine that was leading the parade of celebration in an uproar of ovations and martial music and storms of flowers and she shoved the basket through the window and shouted to her son that since you'll be passing right by take advantage and return these bottles to the store on the corner, poor mother." The "stigma of soli-

tude" can be made bearable only by the transforming imagination, as it was in the tales told García Márquez by his grandparents, as it is in his own inexhaustible capacity for containing these
transformations in language. He abundantly outdoes his origins.
What García Márquez is showing us all the time is the humanizing power of the imagination. In all his writing, the imagination
is no mere whimsey, nor a Latin-American eccentricity: it is a way
of dealing with the mysteries of existence, an essential tool for
survival, as we say nowadays. The people of Macondo live in a
world full of mysteries, without access to any explanation. All
they can count on to make these mysteries bearable is the transforming power of their own imaginations, through the anecdotes
and fictions they construct to bring the world into some kind of
equilibrium, to find some kind of comfort for the separate solitudes it is their fate to inhabit.

For García Márquez, the marvelous, which he equates with the
human, contains the real, and can transform it at will. "They
should take the hens out of their nests when there's thunder so
they don't hatch basilisks," says Benedición Alvarado on her
deathbed, and at once we know where we are. García Márquez
talked to Vargas Llosa about an aunt who haunted the house of
his childhood—the same aunt who sewed her own shroud.
"Once, she was embroidering in the passage when a girl arrived
with a strange-looking hen's egg, an egg with a protuberance,"
he said. "I don't know why our house served as a kind of consulting room for all the mysteries of the place. Every time anything out of the ordinary cropped up, which nobody understood,
they went to the house and asked, and, in the main, this woman,
this aunt, always had an answer. What enchanted me was the
naturalness with which she settled these questions. To go back to
the girl with the egg, she said, 'Look! Why does this egg have a
protuberance?' Then my aunt looked at her and said, 'Ah, because
it is a basilisk's egg. Light a bonfire on the patio.' They lit the fire
and burned the egg as if it were the most natural thing in the

world. I think that naturalness gave me the key to *One Hundred Years of Solitude*, where the most terrifying and extraordinary things are recounted with the same straight face this aunt wore when she said that a basilisk's egg—I didn't know what it was—should be burned on the patio."

Notes from a
Spanish Village

In Spain during the fifties, I would often visit friends who had retreated to a small mountain village, well off the beaten track. The silence was towering, absolute. I got to know the place and its inhabitants; and when I heard of a remote house for sale, well beyond the village, I bought it, and over the next twenty years, I spent a part of each year there. The village had once been self-sufficient, but it was changing, as all Spain was changing. The village became my Spanish microcosm, and in 1974, I wrote the first of a number of pieces from there, chronicling both the quickening pulse of Spain and the village's slow dying. I have pruned the pieces of dated material. From the beginning, I took care not to name or identify the place; and I see no reason to do so now.

These pieces were at the center of a curious storm that blew up in the American press during June of 1984. A year or so before, I had addressed a seminar at Yale University on the wavering line between fact and fiction, using examples from various writers, Borges among them, and from my own work. A student from the seminar went on to become a reporter and published a piece in the *Wall Street Journal* that charged me with having made a practice of distorting facts, quoting the cases I had cited in my seminar. Many newspaper editorials took up the story as though it were fact, and used it to wag pious fingers at the *New Yorker*. A number of columnists reproved me for writing about an "imaginary" Spanish village, a charge that would have delighted the flesh-and-blood inhabitants. The people I wrote about I had known for close to thirty years, in the course of which I had watched babies grow up and marry, and friends grow old and die. I spoke with my friends there almost every day, and some of the conversations I reported I distilled from long acquaintance. Not a single one of my critics, as far as I could judge, had gone back to read the pieces in question.

Summer 1974

It is now more than twenty years since I first came across the village—years in which I have returned to it time after time. I hope I may be forgiven for concealing where in Spain it is and what it is called; since the place and its inhabitants have always stubbornly defended their privacy, I would not violate it for the world. The village lies in the mountains, with a distant view of the sea, and is remote but just accessible. It has endured the staggering changes that have overtaken Spain in that time without being ravaged, as many places were; for me, it has been a mirror of these changes, and it has taught me a great deal. Some years after getting to know the place, and spending different periods of time in it, I bought an abandoned house in the vicinity, high up above the village, in a spot that even the villagers consider remote. In buying the house, I changed from being a visitor without responsibilities to being a preoccupied inhabitant, from looking in from the outside to being on the inside. Besides that, the house's existence added a necessity to returning that had not existed before. I would think about the house, in other places, in other countries, on winter evenings; the thought of a house standing by itself—remote, unoccupied, and unvisited—is strangely perturbing. I bought the house in my son's name, since he was born in Spain and so was able to own property without complications; and we would talk about it, he and I, remembering its sounds, imagining its aura, making lists of things to take there next time, drawing diagrams of alterations we planned to make. It kept Spain in mind for us, and we would pounce on Spanish stories in the newspapers, conscious of the house as an extension of ourselves. Sometimes, on impulse, I would write to our nearest neighbor, a farmer named Eugenio, who kept a key and would look in at odd times, and especially after storms, to see that the house stood sound.

•

You cannot stumble on the village. For one thing, the road ends there, and, for another, you cannot see it from below—not until the church looms above you, and houses begin to show on the carefully groomed terraces, dotted haphazardly here and there, with no apparent access. Around the last, climbing corner, more of the village appears, as though the houses had suddenly shown themselves in order to see who was coming. It is a perplexing place, in that it has no real center except a quiet paved square beside the church. It has grown up among the terraces that line two bowls in the steep side of the valley. Each house appears to have been conceived separately. There are no streets. The paved road becomes a dust road, then a track winding up and up. Above the top rim, the sky is fiercely blue. My son and I have often tried to make a map of the place, but it defeats us; only an aerial photograph would show the curious contours of the ground. We are used to being surprised by the place—by the way each house looks out on a different village, a different-shaped mountain. The mountains set the atmosphere—gray rocky crests hazy in the heat, with a fringe of pines on the tree line and, on the lower slopes, olive groves and long rows of darker-green almond trees. We climb steadily up, with the slow, bent-kneed plod that the villagers use, turning to look down over the village, a patchwork of ochre roofs and green terraces, and then we walk over the crest onto a small, fertile plateau, on the far corner of which stand our house and, beside it, a little ilex forest, which falls steeply away to the next valley, far below. From the house, there is no trace of the village, and no sound other than the jangle of goat bells, or the bark of the dog on the adjoining farm. Sitting on the stone terrace, I can hear insects rustling in the wheat, the whirr of birds' wings, the stirring of leaves. Sounds of our well—the rattling chain, the thud and plunge of the bucket, the creak of the wheel— loom loud in the attention. Over the village hangs the same towering silence. The hollows form acoustical traps, so conversations across the valley will float into hearing, the words just indistinguishable but the tune clear. The sound of an occasional car does

not break the silence so much as puncture it slightly, thus under-
lining it. On still afternoons, we can hear the children singing in
the forest, shepherded by the nuns. The silence is such that we are
careful about breaking it.

•

I first went to Spain in the early fifties, almost by accident—certainly without forethought, for I knew and felt little about the
country beyond a strong antipathy for the Franco regime. I had
not been there very long, however, before it dawned on me that
Spain was going to matter a great deal to me, and become a part
of my life; I found it recognizable at once, in the way that something one has been looking for subconsciously is recognizable.
What caught me so quickly was an energetic sense of immediacy,
a relish for the living moment: when Spaniards sat down at a
table, they instinctively shed any preoccupation other than that
with the food in front of them and with the immediate company.
Their past was too brutal to bear remembering, their future out
of their hands, so they chose to live in a vivid, existential present,
which made conversation easy and open in spite of the pervasive-
ness of the regime. At that time, too, they were delighted by the
appearance of foreigners among them, being curious, hungry for
some notion of a way of life other than their own, because they
had been cut off from other countries from 1936 until 1948 and
longed for anything to break the stalemate of their isolation. The
shame of the Civil War still hung over everything, a brutal ghost,
from whose shadow the people were tentatively emerging.
Doubts remained, however, and the few scattered foreigners who
showed up provided some hope, some positive distraction. The
country was poor and without luxury of any kind, but a simple
dignity abounded, a graceful rhythm that soon had me converted.
I set out to learn and explore as much of Spain as I could—the
language, the terrain, the history, the character. To enter another
culture from choice is always invigorating: we do not have any
habits, so everything catches the attention and becomes grist to

our minds. Not to know the word for, say, soap can be exasperating, but learning it is a small adventure in which the soap glows
momentarily, as though seen for the first time. Even street names
start up trails of discovery. Who was General Goded? Finding out
unravels the whole complex knitting of the Civil War. We discover a new past, wholly different from our own.

·

In the early fifties, Spain had been separated so long from the rest
of the world that to go there felt like moving back through time—
a rare but temporary pleasure. Almost everything was still done
by hand, and the country moved at mule pace. The few cars in
action were ancient models; the taxis dated from the twenties and
thirties. Foreigners who brought their cars to those dusty, unpredictable roads would have to wait to have spare parts fashioned by
amazingly inventive mechanics, and would attract crowds. The
country belonged to its pedestrians. In those days, it was possible
to wander across great squares in the center of cities, like the Plaza
de Cataluña in Barcelona or the Plaza de Cibeles in Madrid, without bothering to look in any direction, for the few passing cars
took pains to keep clear of pedestrians, being in a hazardous minority. That luxurious calm lasted only a short time, however; it
was splintered first by scooters, which began to proliferate in the
early fifties, and soon afterward by the appearance of Spain's first
postwar car, the Biscúter—an amazing creation about the size of
a Dodg'em car, with a lawnmower-sized engine that made a noise
like the continuous popping of corks. The first Biscúters had no
reverse gear but could quite easily be lifted and pointed in a new
direction, provided the passenger dismounted; and the little canvas top, when it was raised, closed with a huge zipper. Biscúters
gave the streets a toy-town air. They were cheerful—laughable,
even—and held no threat, for clearly they could do no harm. I
drove one for a month and had to push it up hills with any degree
of steepness. I often wish the country had settled for them and
kept them, instead of going on to the point where, at present,

Madrid registers the highest rate of vehicular pollution in all Europe, and the outskirts of Barcelona have become a maze of overpasses and six-lane highways. I noticed in the newspapers last summer that vintage-car dealers were offering to buy and sell Biscúters at a price more than ten times what they once cost. No one who putt-putted along in them in those innocent days could ever have imagined that they would arrive at such a state of grace so soon.

•

Communications in the village depend on word of mouth, and are at the mercy of memory. In the store, Doña Anna tells me that Don Anselmo wishes to see me, though she cannot remember when she got the message. At my convenience, she says. But I walk down the spiralling path right away, respectful of the summons. Don Anselmo occupies an extraordinary position in the village—virtually that of headman. Although he has given up being mayor after almost forty years, he is deferred to and consulted regularly, and everywhere he is shown the same reverent respect. Stories about him abound, for from time immemorial he has been called in to arbitrate every kind of dispute, quarrel, or disagreement in the village and its surrounds, and locally his judgments ring as famously as those of Sancho Panza—even among the foreigners, who have often come to him for counsel. A broad, bulky man, he is profoundly ugly, massively ugly, except that his ugliness is easily trounced by the tangible kindness of his look and manner. He owns and runs a small *pensión*, which has the village's only bar and terrace. He bought it, he told me once, so that those who wanted to see him would always know where to find him. Don Anselmo has never bothered much about the *pensión*, except that he likes to do the cooking, and I often talk to him in the kitchen while he is preparing soup or skinning rabbits. The bar is sparse and bare, with family photographs on the walls and a huge stuffed armchair that serves as Don Anselmo's rostrum. I owe to him almost everything I know about the village; he has both a prodigious memory and a voluminous journal and can reach back not only through his own lifetime but practically to the village's coming into being, for his father was mayor before he was, and he claims the ancestral memory as his own. He is not only well informed but endlessly curious; he questions me often about the foreigners—where they come from, what they do, what they feel about the village. Some of them he likes, others he treats with a grave formality.

On the day I got his message from Doña Anna, I found him deep in his chair, gazing into thought, the newspaper unopened on his lap, his face furrowed like a plowed field. "How goes it?" I asked him. "Well enough," he replied. "But my wife has given me all these illustrious articles to read, and it has propelled me to think very much and to wish to consult with you." He waved at a pile of magazines beside the chair, and, picking them up one after another, I found that they were all opened to articles on automobile pollution. I realized what had been happening. Don Anselmo's wife, a bright, birdlike woman, is a great devourer of magazines and serves as a kind of information bank for her husband. Don Anselmo was wearing his prophetic look. "I'm thinking of talking with Guillermo about banning cars from the village." He eyed me speculatively.

"But, Don Anselmo, there are hardly twenty cars in the place!"

"Twenty-two," he corrected me. "And I realize that they affect neither our air nor our chests in any serious way. The only nuisance they do is to come back late and wake up Nicolás in the house by the road. He is old and needs his sleep. No, it is only that I have been reading these learned articles, and I am astonished that in the face of this terrible knowledge not a single town has taken any step to confront the matter. For that reason, I am of the opinion that we must take the step, although we are not in immediate danger. It might lead other places to follow our example. First, I thought I would consult with you over what the foreigners might think. Would they understand? They must certainly be more conscious of this pollution than we are. I intend to talk to them, in any case."

Don Anselmo's plan never quite came to pass, although it preoccupied the village for some time. Were the number of cars to increase, Guillermo announced, they would all have to be left on the level ground below the church. But it is an unlikely prospect. Next year, in accordance with Spanish educational policy, the village school will be closed down and the children taken by bus to a central regional school some thirty kilometers away, in the market town. Those families with children may very well move closer to the school, closer to civilization; some have already made the decision. Don Anselmo, in despair, proposed a voluntary school in the village, for both foreign and local children. "We could have the first multilingual village in all Spain," he announced dramatically, throwing his arms wide. I wish that every one of his plans had come into being.

•

"How could you live in Spain under a dictatorship? Surely there is a moral obligation to stay out?" I used to be plagued by that question, especially in the fifties, but it never troubled me as much as it did the questioner. The refusal of Picasso and Casals to set foot in a Franco-dominated Spain carried a kind of silent thunder; their absence was felt. But few others could make that gesture count, and being in Spain always felt much more like belonging to a conspiracy against the regime than like condoning it. At first, foreigners were cast as liberators, more questioned than questioning, extravagantly welcomed. Their presence did much for the country where, in those days, you could be fined for wearing a bikini or kissing in public; what they did and said and wore at least offered a glimmer of alternatives, an inkling of the outside world. At first, only a few clumps of foreigners came and stayed, for conditions were fairly simple and tourism did not exist. No one could then have imagined the huge assault it became some fifteen years later—to the point where thirty-four-and-a-half million tourists trooped through Spain in 1973, or more than one for every Spaniard. Tourism became the principal national industry and caused the government, which realized that it could not repress Spaniards and attract tourists at the same time, to lift regulations and embark on a cautious liberalization. Even so, there was a price, and Spaniards, having grafted a cheap, cardboard Spain on top of the real one, have only lately awakened to their own corruption. Tourism on a large scale becomes sheer prostitution, as Don Anselmo is fond of saying—and, he adds, prostitutes cannot keep their charms forever. The first signs of such a decline are in the air. Before long, we may see on worn stretches of the Spanish coast new sets of modern ruins—skyscraper hotels with crumbling bars, cracked swimming pools, vines growing up the elevator shafts.

•

Eugenio, who comes to turn over the terraces and cut back the almond trees, tells me the wistful history of the village every year. From its beginnings, the village's main sustenance came from making charcoal and cutting wood to burn, thus fuelling the surrounding countryside. The men would go out from Monday to Friday onto the long wooded slope behind the village, extending halfway up the mountain, to build the careful piles of small wood and twig, which were sealed over except for a small escape at the top. The wood smoldered away, eventually turning into charcoal. For their cooking, the villagers always started the charcoal outside, in a three-legged stove, over a fire of twigs, and then transferred it, red-hot, with tongs, to iron burners set in tile in the kitchen, fanning it with woven-straw fans that the women of the village made in their houses. The women were also very skillful at drying and preserving food for the men to take out with them during the week. The men slept out, and Eugenio showed me a sumptuous sleeping bag he had sewn for himself out of sheepskins, which he never uses now. Around 1958, butane gas in cylindrical containers made its appearance, and in no time *bu-tagas* had transformed the countryside. It was, of course, easier to use than charcoal, but, more than that, it seemed to show that Spain was creeping forward after being stagnant for so long. For the charcoal burners, however, gas meant that their work stopped dead. Most of them were able to find jobs in construction, because the building boom had begun by then; for that, though, they had to leave the village—sometimes for good. It felt as if the place had surrendered all its energy and slumped into disuse. Don Anselmo did his best to animate the place, with schemes to buy looms and to found a pottery, but the villagers had fallen victims to a disheartened listlessness. Besides, by then a handful of foreigners had settled in the place, and work on their houses, or in their houses, kept the village ticking over, in a semiretired kind of way. I still get charcoal from Eugenio, who prepares a pair of burnings every year, but the straw fans have disappeared forever. Don Anselmo remains hopeful. "I can see a time coming when they will be pleading with us to make charcoal again," he says. "Oil and gas will give out, and we shall become an important source, I know it. I have longings to see our village come back to life. That it may still be possible sustains me as I decline." What Don Anselmo never mentions is that the men of the village supplemented their money from making charcoal by picking up and distributing contraband cigarettes, until the contraband traffic dwindled, roughly when the charcoal did. He refuses to hear any mention of contraband. Even his optimism about charcoal he keeps for public occasions; when he talks in private, I can see how thoroughly he has identified the dying of the village with his own dying.

•

After Franco became head of state, his photographic likeness was displayed prominently in all town halls throughout Spain. Every few years, a new photograph was sent around, so that the Spanish people might be suitably attuned to the growth in stature of their little Generalíssimo. As mayor, Don Anselmo received these photographs over the years and duly hung the current likeness in the small office that serves as town hall. He did not, however, destroy the old photographs but kept them carefully. One day, he motioned to me and told me he had something to show me. He led the way along a back corridor, up a few steps, to a locked door, which he opened with a key he produced from his wallet. The room was stale and dusty, entirely empty except for a single straight wooden chair, but around the walls hung, in sequence, a whole row of official photographs of Franco. As my eyes moved slowly along the walls, Franco aged steadily, almost imperceptibly. Don Anselmo put his hand on my shoulder. "I would appreciate that you do not mention this in the village," he said solemnly. "I come here from time to time to meditate on mortality, on the mortality of all of us. I find it curiously comforting. A new picture is due next year, and Guillermo has promised it to me. I have the feeling it may end the series. But I have said that before. Now, let us leave. I feel that at this stage a glass of wine might be appropriate." He locked the door carefully, but the photographs have remained in my head.

·

Tourism washed over the village, leaving it unperturbed, if not untouched. At one time, busloads of tourists used to labor up the road and spill out into the small square, perhaps lured by the prospect of seeing Spain as it once was, but there was nowhere for them to go and nothing for them to do. As often as not, they would find Don Anselmo asleep in his armchair, the priest asleep on his porch, and a pervasive, yawning indifference to their presence—and to their custom, for Don Anselmo runs his *pensión* as an amplification of his house, without thought of profit. A small handful of foreigners live permanently in the village, but either they have chosen the place for its staunch sense of privacy or they are fiercely eccentric—like the Brigadier, who day after day pores over his campaign maps, waiting for the Second World War to resume. Every now and again, someone from the outside world decides that the village is a private Eden, crying out to be shared with an imported elite. We watch with some alarm as the building begins, the mason and the carpenter pitching in with faintly uncomfortable pleasure over having work to hand. But not all ideas of Eden coincide. Prospective buyers come and go, dithering over their decisions. To some, the silence looks alarmingly like total suspension. Refrigerators and swimming-pool filters, moreover, lie far beyond the technological resources of the village, and more than one foreigner has fled the place in despair, the idyll lost for want of a stop valve. The most threatening settler to date was a Swiss woman who envisioned the village as a setting for her own private arts festival, and who whipped up a cluster of small chalets, with pool and performing space, to house her captive celebrities. She goaded and bullied her workmen to the point where she had hired and fired every available hand in the place, earning herself a staggering collection of unrepeatable nicknames. The artists she managed to lure there left after a few days, discovering that they were expected to serve as lapdogs—that their main function was to relieve the boredom of their patroness. Judging by the gleam I notice in local eyes whenever she is mentioned, I would not be surprised to see her houses begin to crumble in the course of the coming year.

•

To come to rest in the village from somewhere in the outside world is not the easiest of transitions, and those who try it occasionally find themselves the victims of "village paranoia." They abuse or assault the mailman, or complain that the phone in the *estanco* is tapped. The victims gradually begin to suffer from their chosen isolation and often conjure up a conspiracy that winds in the whole village, down to its animals and machines. The postman is accused of burning letters or throwing them away, but since he is quite prone to do this, the accusation serves nothing but the paranoia. The villagers treat such an outbreak with uncommon indulgence. They have seen it before and look on it as an unfortunate but inevitable consequence of civilization. But then they are indulgent of any eccentricity, among themselves as well, looking on it as no more than the expression of extreme differentiation. A bald Venezuelan violinist who once lived there, in a solitary house on the crest, had such delusions of social superiority that he insisted that his house be known as the Castle. The villagers not only complied but addressed him in the bar, in the store, in the *estanco*, on the road, as "Your Excellency." Sebastián, who drives the bus to town, stops sometimes at a spot where his grandfather went over the edge and gets out to pray. And when Javier, the shepherd, comes down in the afternoon to sit on the wall outside the *pensión* and carries on a long conversation with his dog, those who pass are careful to greet the dog as well as Javier, whether the dog is there or not. I often get the notion that the villagers look on the foreigners among them as a species of household pet, for I have overheard them on the bus comparing the antics of various foreign households, as excited as if the presence of these strange people were a running comedy, an endless television serial. Only drunkenness turns them cold; any willing surrender of dignity reduces them to a tight silence.

•

Between the late fifties and the late sixties, Spain, which had been noticeably behind the times, burst suddenly into the modern world—or, rather, had the modern world burst on it. Those who knew it even fifteen years ago find themselves wandering around like grandfathers, muttering, "Why, I remember when . . ." In that small compass, the country compressed a century's worth of change, falling greedily on gadgets, plastic, and pieces of extraneous mechanism that had previously appeared only in foreign magazines. Yet between Spaniards and machines a strong antipathy has always existed, and high technology did not settle on Spain without an ungainly honeymoon: new hotels were apt to fall down, swimming pools to leak away, can openers to fail in the breach. The first Spanish supermarkets, too, were more wishful than practical—vast spaces with isolated pyramids of rusty tin cans and, I remember vividly, nothing on the gleaming cold shelf but frozen chicken feet. Before technology, the village all but sustained itself, carting its surplus to market. It even boasted a private electrical system—a local generator that supplied the more central houses but ran solely at the whim and disposition of its master, who would dip it three times before he switched it off at night, to give people time to scuttle for candles. We cooked with charcoal on small iron stoves and warmed ourselves over shallow charcoal *braseros*. Almost everything was done by hand. Sometimes I would take a load of vegetables for my farmer neighbor to the market town thirty kilometers away, setting out at four in the morning with the donkey cart, which maintained a resolute walking pace. The journey takes about half an hour by car but needed four hours with the donkey. The pace seemed ideal, for there was time; I was able to doze off occasionally, or take in every passing tree. Now, however, the donkey carts keep off the roads, and, worse, much of the growing land has been either abandoned for lack of anyone to work it or sold piecemeal to construction companies.

•

For the people of the village, the outside world means the market town, where their vegetables go, where the bigger children are at school, where the young men find work now, and where trouble comes from. Doña Isabel and Doña Matilde, both seamstresses, both in their seventies, have never been there; they do not like what they hear about it, they told me, and they feel no obligation to go. All that comes from the town is a series of officials, decrees, bills, and changes, while they cherish and cling to a notion of the village as self-sufficient, at the center of things. They talk of a time, seemingly legendary but relatively recent, when no one in the place carried money, when food and services were bartered or willingly exchanged, when time did not move forward but turned in the agrarian round. Gathering olives and almonds, whitewashing, baking bread, doing laundry were all communal activities, whereas now, as often as not, the crops go uncollected—the work is no longer worthwhile. Abandoned land, dry fields, unpruned trees are shameful sights to the old ones, to whom good land still means health and wealth. To have surrendered self-sufficiency, they feel, is both tragic and insane. Some years ago, when our house needed a new roof and I had to carry sand and materials along the rocky path, I borrowed a donkey from Doña Isabel—the last donkey left in the village, a patient creature, with mournful eyes, called Carita, who plodded uncomplainingly back and forth. There used to be forty in the place at one time, according to Doña Isabel—"as many as there are *extranjeros* now." Last summer, she told me that Carita had died.

•

At one time the only telephone in the village was in the *estanco*, the store that sells tobacco and stamps in a wooden kiosk set back in one corner, surrounded by wine barrels and sacks of beans. Consuelo, who runs the store, came in from her kitchen drying her hands, put on her spectacles wearily, and cranked the apparatus before asking for a number in Frankfurt or New York, while the caller fidgeted on the sacks. Most of the foreigners have learned the inside of that store by heart at some time or other, because a call either came through with disturbing speed or took the best part of two days. Waiting does different things to callers: some of them rushed from the store in rage or tears; others fell asleep or drank themselves into silence; and one Dutch girl, under Consuelo's tuition, learned the Spanish word for every object in the place. In private, Consuelo complains bitterly about the telephone, for she has to suffer a bleak series of uncomprehending and incomprehensible rages. One year, she was so beset by foreign hysteria in the *estanco* that she pleaded with Don Anselmo to have the telephone removed altogether, and he managed to placate her only by praising her forbearance (she is infuriatingly taciturn) and pointing out that without the unfortunate machine no one would be able to summon the doctor, who lives in the next village (another cause of foreigners' hysteria). Myself, I suspect that Consuelo revels in these long delays—not so much because she wants company in the store as because she has that most Spanish distrust of mechanisms and any dependence on mechanisms. Not without justification do the villagers associate the coming of machines with the coming of foreigners, who did bring in a whole host of pumps, generators, filters, sprinklers, tractors, and assorted vehicles, without which the village had existed quite happily, and all of which made noise. (Spaniards, of course, want all of them or want none of them.) Julián, the nearest we have to a mechanic, does his job with brilliant eccentricity. One day, he fitted an ingenious ratchet stop of his own devising to our well wheel, to take the weight of the bucket; yet he has never made another. He has kept the postman's prewar motorbike running by making spare parts in his shop, but he dislikes new cars and repairs them warily and bizarrely: the Brigadier's car would start only with the glove compartment open after Julián had been at it. "I like to be boss of the machine, even to make it," he once told me. "Machines should be single things. Something is needed? Something is solved. But when the machines all come at me, ready-made and perfect, there is no place for me." I know what he means. Our house remained for years a place of perfect silence, for although we had electricity, we scarcely used it, following the sun instead. Ultimately, however, I bought a refrigerator, which starts up through the night with a thunderous purr. I am waiting for it to break down, so that I can give it to Julián, in the interests of research.

•

The attraction of Spain in the nineteen-fifties lay in its apparent permanence. It was well out of the technological stream, and it had the kind of climate that simplifies physical existence, besides being cheap to live in. Most of all, it had an immemorial look and feel, the landscape bleached and whittled down, the rhythm stark and clear, the style frugal. (Ironic now to realize that those who settled there became, unwittingly, the impulse behind the destruction of that rhythm—but since the dignified frugality of the Spaniards stemmed from poverty and lack, such retrospections are self-indulgent. Only a minority of Spaniards feel, as Don Anselmo does, the loss of that equilibrium as a tragedy.) People strayed to Spain from mixed motives. It served as a mecca for alcoholics, with liquor cheap and available always, just as it attracted would-be bullfighters and flamenco dancers, moths round that antique lamp. Writers and painters dug themselves in quite happily, since they were looking, above all, for time, and Spain seemed as close as anyone could come to a continuum. Yet living there became something of a test, for the simple life, as anyone who has embarked on it must know, can turn out to be insurmountably complicated in its mechanics, and quite often sends would-be villagers screaming back to civilization. To set up a small, self-contained world, ignoring the surrounding currents, proves too much for all but a few hardened eccentrics. Those who settled in Spain in small, elitist groups suffered the isolation of castaways: the silence drummed on the roof like rain, and news from home became the only reality. A clear distinction has to be made between tourists, expatriates, and foreigners. Tourists descend on a place in obedient droves, like migrant birds, either following well-beaten tracks or creating them for other tourists. For them, to be in a foreign country is a change, a difference, a chosen astonishment. Above all, their stay is, by definition, temporary and pleasure-bent. Spaniards regarded tourists as a badge of well-being and economic health until they began arriving on a seemingly endless belt, forcing the country to feed, fuel, and amuse them at a thoroughly un-Spanish rate. For once, the fatalism of the Spaniards served them badly: their hospitality lost them their house. Expatriates behave quite differently. They have left their own countries on a long lead, never quite severing the link with home, never quite adapting themselves to their exile, clinging to one another for company, haunting post offices, magazine stands, and banks, waiting expectantly for money from home, anything at all from home. Expatriates are generally getting their own countries into perspective, to the point where they feel strong enough, or desperate enough, to return to them. Foreigners, conversely, live where they are, leaving their pasts and countries behind them for the place they take root in. In one sense, they are lucky: they are free to enter a new context unencumbered, with clear eyes, and are often able to savor a place in a way that escapes the inhabitants, for whom it has become habit. But however well a foreigner adapts himself to a place and its inhabitants, however agile he becomes in the lore and language, there is a line he can never cross, a line of belonging. He will always lack a past and a childhood, which are really what is meant by roots.

•

The real frontier to cross is that of the language. The Spaniards themselves are not famous with other languages—not as linguistically accommodating as, say, the Dutch, who can shift languages imperturbably. They do, however, have great linguistic kindness, in that anyone with a minimal supply of Spanish discovers conversations being put together for him, being turned into small language lessons for his benefit. At first, Spanish is an easy language to enter—regular, uncomplicated, straightforward to pronounce—and most foreigners who settle in Spain quickly acquire a form of "kitchen" Spanish, which allows them to shop, ask directions, go to banks and offices, and order in restaurants. However, that stage may well become a plateau on which they stay, enacting formal conversations, the language technically accurate but without much emotion. Germans probably speak the most wooden Spanish of all, striding through sentences and subduing them one by one, while the English wield it with a mixture of distaste and disbelief, as though not sure it will work. But so kind are Spaniards that their talk will often limp along in sympathy with any stranger making heavy weather. In the village, this comes to be something of a problem; Joaquín, the mason, for instance, has done so much building for newcomers to the language that when he is explaining anything he cannot help breaking into a kind of baby talk, which his workers now all imitate. Don Anselmo's wife is often pressed to give language lessons, but she is so energetic that she has acquired three extra languages over the years while her pupils floundered about in chapter I of *Don Quixote*. Not that language is insurmountable. Little Doña Anna, who in her store has to confront shopping lists in Finnish as a matter of course, has evolved a series of elaborate mimes for recipes and foodstuffs, which bring extra-linguistic results—prodigious performances from hungry aliens, who circle balletically round plump Doña Anna, waving arms and drawing animals and vegetables in the air. The greater hazards arise with those who cannot bear to undergo the embarrassment of learning a new language, and pretend to know it or, at least, to subdue it. We have one such eccentric settler, who after some years believed that Spanish had descended on him by osmosis. Whenever Spanish was directed at him, he would nod vigorously and say, "*Sí, sí, sí!*" It served him well enough until one day Joaquín came to replace a tile in his roof. When the mason had finished, he gesticulated at the roof and made a small emphatic speech in Spanish, to which our neighbor replied with his usual "*Sí, sí, sí!*" A couple of days later, he came back from the town to find his house being completely reroofed and Joaquín and his men beaming at him enthusiastically.

•

All languages have a particular feel to them, for they embody a mode of being, a cast of thought, a musical manner. Some slip on more easily than others and are more comfortable to wear. But the wearer must inevitably yield to them, because languages are strangely demanding. I knew no Spanish when I first went to Spain, and learned it slowly until I was stung by the necessity of talking to people about more than weather and well-being. Necessity prompts even more assiduously than curiosity. Then I found myself not just learning Spanish but being changed by it, behaving differently in it. For one thing, Spanish is a more extravagant and spontaneous language than English and must be delivered with a precise vocabulary of gestures; now I gesticulate while speaking English. Spanish proved liberating, in a way; I found I could grow vociferously angry with much more ease in Spanish than in English, and I fell into making proverbial utterances, as Spaniards do, just because they serve the language almost as punctuation. I loved the language and still love it; equally, I am still learning it. To come late to another language means that even after it is learned well some of its dimensions are lacking. One is that of its written past, its literature and mythology; and it takes a discouragingly slow trudge to catch up. But what remains always out of reach is the experience of having known a language as a child, when words were intuitively calculated rather than learned; that instinctive knowing is what underlies wordplay, wit, and word music, the sudden surprises that can happen in language, that extend language. A friend from Peru remarked on the same thing while he was learning English: "I can read all the nursery rhymes, discover what they mean, but I can never get to the state of feeling them before their meaning, when the words are acting like a spell. I can have no past in the English language." Translating back and forth between the two languages, I often find myself with a foot in each, conscious of how great the gap can sometimes be, how distinct the styles; but I accommodate them both, and am grateful for the Spanish extension.

•

In the course of summer, friends come to visit, and once they have got over their first awe of air and silence, tried their hand at drawing water, wielded hoe and spade, made their own solitary forays to Doña Anna's store to bone up on her vast and complex lexicon of gestures (returning on occasion with unlikely pur-

chases but delighted nevertheless with the exchange of extra-linguistic good will), they find their own crowded worlds receding
and get used to drowsing away the afternoons in a hammock in
the ilex forest, attempting to sketch the asymmetrical bulk of the
mountain that looms behind us, reading the books I surely now
know by heart, and in general reducing their lives to a rhythm
that other modes of civilization have made impossible. Some of
them come with a firm intention of mastering Spanish, step by
step, hour by hour, but the rhythm of our village is not one that
makes for the pursuit of firm intentions, and over the years I have
inherited an impressive collection of Spanish grammars. With
time, the outside world does subside and diminish, and the visitors fall in with the rhythm of the sun, waking and sleeping in
accordance with a natural order, not with their own. It comes
more easily to some than to others—than to those, say, who have
turned the ringing of the telephone into a natural sound and grow
anxious in its absence. To settle down in the village is a conversion
of a kind, and although I am practiced at it by now, it still takes
time, because one is rooted forever in two worlds, and for some
people the simplification that village existence requires may be—
however desirable—forever impossible.

•

Below the house, thickly overgrown and by now scarcely distin-
guishable from the undergrowth, stand the walls of seven houses,
their roofs long gone. We often walk among the ruins, for they
exude silence like a message and give an odd aura to everything—
the mountains hazy through the window sockets, the toolmarks
on the stone, the rusted iron rings in the walls. The goats eye us
indignantly, their bells clanking as they withdraw to the end of
their tethers. We have used some of the tumbled stones from the
ruins in laying a stone terrace, embedding them in the ground
with their flattest surfaces uppermost—a caveman's jigsaw puzzle. We have been given the history of the houses many times. At
the turn of the century, they, along with our house and the ad-

joining farm, formed a separate, self-sustaining *aldea*, a small village of close to two hundred people; indeed, I have seen it marked on survey maps of the time—a round, emphatic dot. The story of its decline is a recurring one in Spain: the young people moved to the larger village below; there were not enough hands to attend to crops and animals and maintenance; the old people were left alone with the children; the place faltered, failed, and was abandoned. The house we occupy would have been one of the ruins by now if we had not shored it up, but, with the ruins below, it is not hard to feel like a castaway or a survivor. Once, I came back to the house after a hiatus of two years to find that the vegetation had marched tall across the terrace and was fingering the front door. I felt I was just in time. Sitting beside the well on an evening of silk dark, with stars crowding the sky, I find it easy to imagine the village without any human presence whatever—all signs soon consumed by inexorable vegetal muscles, the fruit thudding to the ground unheard. We are the most strident and extravagant species on the whole planet, but not the most durable, as the ruins keep saying. The house feels more and more like an outpost; the insects and the plants have designs on it. I hope sooner or later to make peace with them.

•

Christmas 1975

A letter comes, in midwinter, from Eugenio's wife, Josefa, enclosing some forms to sign and asking about seed for the spring sowing. Less rain has fallen than usual; they are very much preoccupied with drought. The village is quiet; nothing has happened except that old Nicolás has died. (Poor old Nicolás. He had sat outside every day for years watching the road, as though his death might arrive by the next car.) And then she adds, "*Ya sabemos que la vida es esto: nacer, sufrir, y morir.*" To be born, to suffer, and to die—I cannot believe that the sentence is anything but a formality on her part, because she is a brisk and joyful person, without a trace of melancholy in her bones. And yet it is precisely that fundamental sense of life as fate that gives Spaniards their flinty durability, their unquestioning acceptance of whatever happens to them. They are not speculative by nature. If a choice looms in their lives, they prefer to wait until it is resolved by circumstance. It is this disposition that divides them forever from the foreigners—that keeps the foreigners from being able to belong in any profound sense. From the villagers' point of view, the very fact that the foreigners can choose—choose to leave the village and go elsewhere, choose their own circumstances, change their minds—moves them to another plane of existence. Still, the villagers do not see such choice as particularly desirable; their own existences are comparatively straightforward. What needs doing gets done. What happens happens. The village endures, and within that context of permanence pleasure occurs in the form of happy accidents. As a result, the village is totally without drama other than the dramas of birth, illness, and death. Quarrels are buried and seethe in silence; formality keeps the place running. (The history of the Civil War in rural Spain is more one of paying off old scores than one of ideological conflict.) The only expression of strong feelings I have heard in the village has been the blowing of the conchs. Should any local woman recently widowed entertain the attentions of a suitor too soon for the village's sense of morality, conch shells are blown in her direction at twilight. Nobody in particular blows them. They are blown. Nothing more is said. That eerie wail upholds the village sense of propriety, without confrontation. The conchs, however, would never be blown in the direction of a foreigner, since foreigners, the villagers know well, march to batteries of different drums. Whatever drama is lacking in the place is amply provided by the foreigners; and yet, except in extreme cases, the villagers suspend judgment. A taxi summoned in the middle of the night, a crash of breaking glass or furniture from the Venezuelan's house, a distracted phone call—they are used to such events by now, and the dramas of the foreigners have as little to do with their lives as the *tele-novelas* they watch disbelievingly in the *pensión*.

•

At the end of 1975, I flew to Spain from Geneva. I had written ahead to Josefa, telling her I was coming, so that she would leave the keys in their accustomed place, under a stone in the old bread oven. Her scrupulously arranged bouquet would be on the table, wood would be stacked, and a fire would be laid. I looked forward to footstepping through that powerful silence, to putting on the perspectives of the place with the old work coat that would be hanging on its wooden peg. The plane was full of Spaniards, bright-faced and gift-bearing, expansive at the prospect of going home. (Spaniards have always seemed to me far and away the gloomiest of exiles, perpetually wistful, haunted by longings for their homeland. I sat beside a woman from the Alpujarras, who told me that after twenty years of working in Switzerland she still could think of that country only as a kind of game or mechanism that gave her the chance of saving enough to buy a house in her pueblo, a house she dreamed of in snow-deep Swiss winters.) What was preoccupying me was the prospect of setting foot for the first time in a Spain without General Franco, and the first thing I did after landing and threading my way through policemen, customs, and squealing relatives was to buy an armful of Spanish newspapers and reviews, to replace the yellowing ones left in the house from the last visit. The sunset was reddening the mountains, but it was still light enough on the bus ride to town to make out old landmarks among the new—the glassblower's and the bookbinder's shouldered aside by shining supermarkets, and by spacious, well-lit filling stations that had begun by being solitary pumps. In town, the air smelled of the harbor, briny and brisk in the nose. The café tables had moved inside for the winter, and the lottery sellers were gloved and scarved. To set foot in Spain always brings on a tingle of pleasure; I can feel my whole manner change with my language. I made my way to a bar where the people from the village often forgather, to see if I could pick up a lift instead of dickering with a taxi-driver, who would swear he had never heard of the village. Inside the steamy café, I saw Sebastián, our bus driver, expostulating by the bar. We back-slapped our greetings and went through all the ritual exchanges of meeting again. Yes, he was driving up; he had the truck; if I wouldn't mind making a stop on the way, he had to pick up a pig. Manolo, the carpenter's son, he told me, who was to turn twenty-one the day before Christmas, had been offered by his parents the choice between a television set and a pig. To everyone's astonishment and delight, he had plumped for the pig. Sebastián picked it up, grunting and snuffling in a sack, from a *finca* beyond the cemetery; and over the remaining twenty kilometers he brought me up to date on the village. No, nobody had died, he thanked God, but the priest was being more of a nuisance than usual, forever calling meetings—on cold nights, too. At last rain had fallen, I ought to find my *cisterna* full. Little Elena was having a baby; it would be the first born in the place for more than three years. I would not believe how the prices had risen; the cheapest thing to live on was cognac. As we whined up the winding road, I felt sorry for the pig in the back of the truck, but it had stopped squealing by the time Sebastián put me down at the foot of the steep path. Deciding to postpone visits until the next day, I climbed up to the ridge with my bag and papers, stopping there to look back down on the houses straggling round the terraces below. Windows glowed and chimneys smoked, and the priest had managed to fasten an illuminated star to the church tower. I could hear the bells of sheep I could not see, but nothing else moved or sounded. Under an enormous velvet sky studded with stars, I took the tufted, rocky path to the house.

•

I rise at first light, shivering at the initial touch of the tile floor, to verify the place by daylight, first rattling the bucket into the well for water, then starting the fire with olive chips from Josefa's woodpile. The fig trees and the vine are skeletons of their leafy, summer selves, but as the sun comes up I notice that already three of the almond trees have put out little buttonholes of white blossom. Winter gives the house, the terraces, and the stone walls a bare, bony look, but the sun warms as it climbs, reflecting circles of wavering light from the well bucket on the rough wall. I climb to the small study, looking for signs of leaks in the roof, but the books are dry, with the silence of going long unopened, and a half-written postcard lies on the desk. Dust, but no damp; but still the smell of emptiness, which will take a day or two to lift. Later, I will go down to the village, to find friends, to buy food in Doña Anna's cluttered store. Now I settle on the terrace with the newspapers. I have no idea what time it may be.

•

Someone whistles. I look up. Eugenio has been cutting brush on the ridge and has noticed the smoke from the chimney. We wave, and soon he comes across, climbing the terrace walls—·a little brown, wrinkled man, nimble as a lemur. I could not guess his age within fifteen years. He is delighted to see the house occupied, and he begins to show me what he has done in my absence, and what needs attention—a crack in the gutter, the gate to the forest broken. Would he take some wine? No, just water from the well; he has a long day ahead. And would I do him the favor of allowing him to crop the top of a spruce for a Christmas tree? Of course, my house is his house, as he knows. Rituals of greeting, which must be reenacted again and again in the village, for they keep us all in our places. Our village has been lucky in that the foreigners have remained in a minority and have upset neither its rhythm nor its morality. I watch Eugenio climb quickly up and decapitate the spruce. He is gloomier than ever about his losing battle with the land—he can no longer count on even occasional help from his sons and has been forced to leave most of it fallow, turning instead to turkeys and sheep. What hopes does he have of the new government, I ask him. "Oh, I hope. I cannot think they would be foolish enough to go on ignoring the land. There is much talk of subsidies. But I have never believed that you can bribe people to cultivate the land; it must be in your bones, and my bones are tired." I collect a basket and walk down with him. Josefa, his wife, sits sewing in the sun. More greetings, Eugenio nodding and bobbing all the time. Their son wants them to leave the village and move to a new apartment in town, but they will not hear of it. Josefa clucks indignantly at the idea and shoos away a turkey with her apron. Oh, and had I heard the story about young Manolo and the pig? I was to hear it several times again in the course of the day, in embellished detail.

•

In winter, the village hibernates, waiting for the world to warm up; that makes it easier to find people in their houses, crouching beside fires and stoves, taking occasional survivors' trips to the store. Spain is a sunstruck country, its winters gray, unacknowledged interludes. The local people still go on pretending, to themselves as much as to anyone else, that winter does not happen. Ask them to lay in enough wood for the cold weather and they will come up with a pitifully small bundle, assuring you it will be enough to last for two winters. When it runs out in a matter of weeks, they will shake their heads in wonderment and declare that the climate is changing, it must be because of the *bomba atómica*, that this surely must be the coldest winter since before the Civil War—*nuestra guerra*, our war, as they always call it. In winter, clouds sometimes creep down over the plateau, turning the adjoining mountains into ghosts. When the great rains fall, gushing into the cisterns and turning the paths into quagmires, not a soul will be in sight anywhere. I would not choose to spend the winter here unless I were, say, a watch repairer or were undertaking a definitive translation of the works of Lope de Vega; or unless, of course, I belonged here and tuned in instinctively to whichever rural odd jobs the season requires.

But even that agrarian rhythm has been broken by now—good land lies idle for want of men to work it, or has been sold, or is used only for grazing. The drift to the town, for work or for schooling, has already depleted the place, turning it into a week-end retreat and a haven for reclusive strangers, its population of under a hundred a skeleton crew, a care-and-maintenance party. I can see why the elders in the village were so pleased with young Manolo for choosing the pig over the television set; but it is a choice against the run of time.

•

I shop in Doña Anna's store, as much by instinct as anything, for the contents have changed neither in place nor in character—only in price, she tells me, wringing her hands or rubbing them. Patiently, she enters my purchases in a notebook, muttering over the addition. A heavy snoring comes from the room adjoining the store—her husband, back from his early morning run to the market. "Do the prices go up like this where you live?" she asks me suddenly, and I reassure her. Characteristically, she has no idea of the provenance of any of the foreigners in the village; she simply accommodates them all, even when they can shop only by pointing. Over the fireplace she has tacked a magazine cover of King Juan Carlos and Queen Sofía. "I remember when we had a king before—Alfonso XIII," she confides to me. "But somehow it's difficult to get used to again—saying '*Viva el rey*' after all this time."

•

When, after a ghoulish month of medical agony, Franco did die, I pinned the newspaper headline to the wall, to give the fact time to dawn on me. Franco's death was much more than a single event. It implied the possibility of change at last in the stagnant air of Spain, after almost forty years of stasis. I had never known Spain without Franco's muffling supervision, except in my reading, and I always had trouble connecting its turbulent, energetic, and productive past with the stalemate of its present. All at once, with Franco's dying, Spain again acquired the future, suspended for so long. And though the future—in the newspapers, in conversations—remained as speculative as before, it had moved out of the realm of pure imagination, where Franco had been careful to keep it. This has made Spain curiously watchful, curiously mortal. At a stroke, it has restored involvement. The round little profile still shows on the coins, but coins are objects. The people in Spain who used to say, "How can he last?" now ask themselves in bewilderment, "How could he have lasted? How could we have let him?" To find the answer to that question may provide an essential expiatory labor for the Spanish people for years, in overcoming their own paralysis. No other head of state in our time can have been so much judged from the outside and yet so impervious to the judgments of others. From the moment Franco was declared Head of the Spanish State, in Burgos, in October of 1936, he identified Spain's destiny with his own, obviously convinced that he held power by divine right and was answerable to nobody on earth. That conviction was so strong in him as to make him contemptuous of his enemies, contemptuous of opposition. I can never forget the speech he made on November 22, 1966, when he introduced his Organic Law of the State to the Spanish people like a tart headmaster. "Let all Spaniards remember," he said then, "that every nation is always beset by its familiar demons, different from one country to another. Spain's are: a spirit of anarchy, negative criticism, lack of solidarity among her people, extremism, and mutual enmity." He added that no nation so haunted could expect to govern itself. But these demons had been set loose by Franco himself and his crusade, and it was he more than anyone who kept them alive.

•

Through the glass door of the café I catch sight of Gonzalo, the mailman, and I go in pursuit of him, for he is famously elusive and, I suspect, secretly disapproves of mail. He is not only the mailman but an itinerant gardener, and in the village they will tell you with great mirth how, while he works, he is prone to park a bundle of letters in the fork of a tree, where they will be found years later, wound round with growing ivy. Scratching himself gloomily, he leads me to his office and produces a handful of letters and two telegrams, all long out of date. He is a hoarder of unopened letters, a renowned inducer of paranoia. This time, he is more disgruntled than usual. "Nine newspapers a day used to come to this village," he tells me, "and nobody minded when they got them. Now I have to deliver thirty every day, and magazines besides, and everybody pursues me. Why can't they listen to the radio?" I walk back to the café in the glinting sun and find Don Anselmo in his armchair, newspapers all around him. For years, he has worried about the fate of the village, having seen it dwindle from a healthy, settled community that thrived on agriculture and charcoal-making for fuel (not to mention contraband) to a skeletal place populated mainly by the old, its terraces uncultivated, its trees uncared for, and some of its houses sold to foreigners or to Spaniards from the city. At Christmas, most of these houses are shuttered and dark, their scattered swimming pools filled with green slime. Only a few hardened settlers stay the year round—people who have burned their bridges, painters obsessed with the light, hopeful novelists, refugees from their old lives, waiting for the mail and dreaming of cities. For the local people, they form a captive layer in the village, cared for like communal village pets, nicknamed, talked about. But they adapt in different ways, to different degrees. For some, the village remains a setting into which they fit themselves with all the trappings of their former lives, brushing aside the language and becoming sturdy custodians of their own habits, like the few resolute English, who walk their dogs, fetch their out-of-date newspapers, and have supplies of tea sent out to them. Others adapt with zeal, learning local lore and dialect, to create for themselves what they are missing; namely, a past in the place. I used often to brood on the possibility of living there all the year round, but I decided I could do so only if I were to plunge into the business of working the land and living by an agrarian calendar. Eugenio always encourages me, for he tells me that on most days he finds himself the only person moving in the vast landscape—a mournful experience; but he clearly expects me to turn up with half a dozen able-bodied helpers, for nothing less would rouse the stony terraces from their present sloth. No matter how close we foreigners come to the village and the villagers, however, life there can never take on for us the inevitability it has for them. There is always for us the choice of going somewhere else—a choice they have never entertained.

•

There are just two occasions in the year when the whole village assembles itself—one during its own fiesta, in September, the other on Christmas Eve, for the eleven-thirty Mass. From the top of the ridge, on the way down, I can hear the tiny notes of shouting and laughter being struck in the crowded little plaza far below. The moon is up, and the mountains look like silver-gray cutouts against the star-crowded sky. On the way down, I hear music coming from somewhere—perhaps an itinerant Jehovah's Witness shunning the church. Across the plaza, the door of the church and that of the café face each other, and there is a continuous coming and going between the two. The little priest is helping a group of children dressed as shepherds to tie their leggings. This is his night, and he is everywhere at once, ushering groups of people who are going nowhere, unctuous and censorious at once. The men are in the café, flushed and stiff in their suits. Don Anselmo is in his armchair, wearing a large red tie. He lifts a hand. Have I heard the new audio equipment the priest has bought for the church? I have indeed; as I passed the church door, it was playing, unaccountably, "Jingle Bells." Have I heard the king's speech? I have. Well, at least he said he was aware of the difficulties. Don Anselmo scratches his head and grimaces. The priest is ringing the bell, but no one appears in any hurry to go in. During the Mass, they drift back and forth between the church and the café, greeting one another, slapping one another on the back; for there is not much difference between the two places except for the presence of the priest, who is conducting Mass with his new microphone in one hand, like an ecclesiastical pop singer. Manolo is behind the bar in the café, waiting for Don Anselmo to take over from him. I congratulate him, and he leans toward me. "I suppose you've heard the story," he says in a low voice. "Well, to tell you the truth, I've been saving for a television set myself, and I have the money, so that's why I chose the pig. But don't tell anybody. I've become a hero. Don Anselmo keeps offering me cognac. I think I'd better put off buying the television set for a month or two." He grins. Someone has left a baby behind the bar and it begins to cry. Manolo crosses to the Mass to find its mother. Don Anselmo comes back, takes off his shoes, and beams at everyone. Mass ends, but nobody goes home—it is a chance to shake everybody's hand. As I walk up to the house after saying good night some seventy times, the laughter is still tinkling below; and, just as I reach the ridge, the priest switches out his star.

•

In the week following Christmas, I discover just how much the village has altered in the post-Franco era. Don Anselmo's café, once the exclusive province of the elders and a convenient place to leave messages or baskets, has become the center of a running forum on Spain's future. Papers and magazines are devoured and exchanged, and people I have never seen there before appear and listen to the conversation. Don Anselmo has assumed the role of patient instructor, and one afternoon I hear him deliver a long lecture on the pitfalls of the Spanish constitution. He is at his most expansive, however, when he is welcoming a visitor from another village—a mayor or ex-mayor whom he has invited—cooking the lunch with unusual care. (He is a benevolent cook but not a careful one.) He and his visitor eat together privately and seriously, for all the world like ambassadors from allied coun-

NOTES FROM A SPANISH VILLAGE

tries—or heads of government, for that matter—and then they sit in the café most of the afternoon. I stop in while he is entertaining Gaspar, the mayor of a village on the other side of the mountain—a favorite haunt of foreigners, who present Gaspar with problems quite un-Spanish in nature. He is a cheerful bantam of a man, but he is looking crestfallen today. "I always envy this village," he tells me. "It's kept its proportions. Not like us. For over twenty years now, we've been living because of the foreigners. We sell them houses and then rebuild them; we feed the foreigners, we work for them—there's hardly anyone left in our village who does not work for the foreigners. I won't say things have been easy for us, but I've come to know a number of foreigners quite well over the years—very *simpático*; they kept us alive, not just by settling in the village but by keeping us in touch with the world when we were otherwise screened from it, by showing us different ways to live, some ways we don't particularly want." I feel sorry for Gaspar, because his village, lying in a natural amphitheatre of mountains, has always looked the perfect setting for Mediterranean ritual drama, and so has induced some of the foreigners who settled there to give themselves up to the demands of the landscape, producing a series of scandals that has made the village notorious in the region, and turning Gaspar into something of a rural psychiatrist.

•

I never like leaving the village, perhaps because it is only too easy to imagine the place continuing to exist without me—indeed, without anyone at all—for I have never got over feeling an intruder in that landscape of trees and silence. Don Anselmo's car is going to town early this morning, so I rise while the dawn is no more than a graying in the sky and take a last look around, touching familiar objects, before closing the books, the well, and the house, and leaving the keys under the stone in the bread oven for Josefa. As I pass the farm, the rooster starts up, as he does at anyone's passing, and the dog growls in his sleep. Don Anselmo is waiting just inside the door of the café, in a long nightgown and the majestic dressing gown of a Ruritanian general. He is not going to town, Manolo is driving his car instead and will take me. Is there anything Don Anselmo wants from the outside world, I ask him. "Yes. Send me the clippings from your newspapers about Spain. My wife can translate them for me. And there will be a lot more to talk about when you come next. Remember, my village is your village."

I got into the car beside Manolo, who looked still asleep. As we left, the sun came up suddenly, over the shoulder of the mountain, and Manolo slowly came to life. He asked me a flood of questions about wages and prices in other countries, and I could see his mind racing. I had not seen him the previous year, and he told me he had worked for a chef in a hotel kitchen in France and was now under-chef in a restaurant in town. What would he do next, I asked him. Travel? "No. I didn't much like *living* in France, though the work was satisfying. I noticed one thing—our pay was not so bad, but for the first time in my life I felt poor. Now, I've never felt poor in the village. Not rich, either, although my father always has work. But there's nothing we need, I've never felt deprived of anything, never wanted anything badly that we couldn't have. I owe a lot to Don Anselmo, too. I've worked in his café since I was twelve, and I've heard him talk so many times; and he's taught me a lot about the village—its past, politics, everything. My plan is to gain two more years of experience in the town and then open a restaurant in the village, for ourselves as much as for anyone. Don Anselmo cooks just as an excuse to talk. I would like to cook for the pleasure of it. I like doing that better than anything else I can think of. It would also be keeping the village alive, in a way." I told him I looked forward to that day, thinking of the Spartan diet of beans, fruit, and cheese I usually live on there. We talked about the strikes in Madrid, the foreigners, odds and ends, until the ugly, half-built suburbs began to loom up. "I've been thinking about that pig again," Manolo said suddenly, "and I'm not sure that I chose it just because I was planning to get a television set for myself. I'm not that crazy about watching television, even though there should be more to watch quite soon. No, I think I really wanted that pig. After all," he said, lifting both hands from the wheel, "there can't be many places left in the world where you'd get a live pig for your birthday, but, wherever they are, they must be good places."

•

Summer 1979

At first sight in summer, as the bus grinds its way up through a gap in the mountains, the village looks plump and abundant, like someone who has regained health and girth. I last saw it in an early January, huddled and rain-streaked, with a few doleful faces haunting the windows, but in summer it throws open its shutters and honeys itself in the sun. In Spain, winters are looked on as an unnatural interim, summer as true being. It is easier to find a patch of shade in summer than a pool of warmth in winter. Under the unvarying sun and blue sky, the village surfaces from its hibernation and prepares to take in strangers. Alien cars drive into the dusty plaza beside the church, but their occupants, after wandering around in search of a welcome, soon drive away, apparently puzzled by the silence. Judas, Don Anselmo's dust-colored Alsatian, who is slumped in the shade of a plane tree, opens one orange eye and closes it again. The silence so saturates the place that sounds enter the ear separately and singly—the squeal of an unoiled wheelbarrow, the thunk of an axe from a higher terrace, a girl singing in an unseen garden. June rain has made the place greener than usual, and the vines, already grape-heavy, hang thick over the doorways. I push through the rattling chain fly curtain into the cool of the café. Nobody is there, and nothing has changed—wet-ringed marble bar, dusty wax flowers, messages spiked on an ancient nail, yellowed calendars and pawed photographs, spilled dominoes, deflated newspapers. A wasp is buzzing the top of a dusty *anís* bottle, sounding the note of the sleeping afternoon. Looking across the terrace, I can see the mountain sailing among passing clouds, folded in on itself, gray stone, dark green pine. I hear a noise from Don Anselmo's room and put my head in. He is asleep in his enveloping armchair, his large head on his own shoulder, his breathing like an organ bellows. It would be unthinkable to wake him. Besides, there is plenty of time—the summer feels like a vast, unmoving reservoir of it. As I leave, Judas does not even bother to open his eye.

•

I trudge up to the house, through asphodel and wild fennel waist-high. It is hidden at first in almond foliage; in actuality it is much more reassuring than in memory. Josefa has left the keys in the stone bread oven, by ritual arrangement. She tells me often that just after the turn of the century her parents baked bread in that oven for the small, vanished village from which my house has survived. The only traces of those days are seven ruins below us, their walls clawed at by vegetation. The key thunders in the lock; I am appalled by my own noise. The house has been lately occupied by friends and does not hold the dusty silence that thickens after long isolation. Then it is like entering a cobweb. Dumping my extraterrestrial bag, I wander from room to room (though there are only three rooms) checking objects against my memory, which is always proved to be faulty by the surprise of a stone jar, a hanging lantern. The house looks curiously rearranged, through other people's eyes, but I am in no hurry to shift it. In a few days, it will take on its summer shape. I look over the books in disbelief; they are a kind of jetsam, too miscellaneous to be called a library—visitors, as I am. I do not so much unpack as conceal the things I have brought with me. As a rule, they are not needed until I am ready to leave. I drag a chair out to the terrace and take stock. Eugenio has obviously been about, for the vine is gravid, flaming red flowers star the pomegranate trees, roots have been dusted, the garden cleared, the loquat tree crutched upright. I can think of nothing that needs doing. The roof casts a knife-edge of shadow across the terrace. I watch it. It does not move. Yet when I look again it is somewhere else, farther along. So will the summer go.

•

No one comes to the house by accident, for it is the extreme end of the road. The ilex forest ends in a cliff with a fall of about five hundred feet to the floor of the valley. Not all visitors even find their way to the house. The most surprising visit of the whole summer was that of a meter reader from the electric company. A ponderous knocking just after the sun came up, and I found on the terrace this small uniformed man with a clipboard. He had not read the meter in two years. But he told me he always came to the house, even when he knew it was empty, for he liked to sit in the forest and eat his lunch. I told him, in the manner of the country, that my forest was his forest. But the first person to materialize is always Eugenio. He is generally working nearby, and as soon as he sees a shutter open or hears the plunk of the bucket in the well he sets course for the house. He is small and nimble, like a slow squirrel, and nut-brown with the sun. Nobody I have asked can tell me how old he is—"seventy or something" is the nearest I have got. He farms the land around the ruins, about thirty scattered plots, on which he grows a sumptuous variety of fruit, vegetables, and cereals; and since my land adjoins his, his green influence is now spreading across my terraces. He is permanently happy in his work, for he constantly expresses a mixture of awe and enthusiasm over the fact that things grow. Will he take a glass of wine? Yes, this time he will, but we have to carry it round with us, he is impatient to show me what he has done: the almond trees all pruned, the vines sprayed and yielding double this year, the forest fenced adequately enough for him to quarter his sheep there some nights—good for the undergrowth, too. He farms by instinct—he is not aware of knowing what he knows. He can show you where to make the cut on the almond branch but not why. He has told me the history of the house, down to the last tree. At one point, it was occupied by a fiery citizen who directed contraband in the region, and the ilex forest served then as a way station. Eugenio often tells me with glee how as a young man he would lead a mule from close to the coast up a concealed trail to our forest, through the night, and then cache its cargo of cigarette crates in the three caves in the cliff face just behind us. He is a presence—the only sound I hear apart from the sheep bells is the scrape of his hoe from somewhere below the house, and I sometimes catch sight of him on the ridge, piling brush to block a hole in the wall where the stones have fallen and are unlikely to be replaced. I count him a lucky presence.

·

Eugenio breaks the silence; and from that first encounter the circles of involvement start up and widen. Sooner or later, I collect a basket and set out for the village. Below the small plateau, the houses are so spread and scattered over the groins and outcrops of the mountainside that only an aerial photograph would properly show where they lie in relation to one another. For that reason, one plans descents in advance, threading visits on a string of intention to avoid having to retrace mountainous steps. In winter, a fair number of the houses are sealed, their shutters like blind eyes; but in summer they all show signs of life—chairs on the terrace, towels on the line, intermittent music, isolated voices, a dog barking. I can tell the sound of the mailman's motorbike from other motors. Someone was ruthless enough, three summers since, to bring in a chain saw, the first whine of which brought everybody outdoors in horror. After three days, it fell silent, mysteriously, forever.

·

Eugenio's wife, Josefa, was born in the house and has looked after it for years as though it were a shrine, appearing after storms to see if perhaps a tile on the roof has loosened. Lately, she has taken to eking out Eugenio's seasonally variable profits by looking after the empty houses of the more affluent (and consequently more absent) foreigners, and this activity makes her the most difficult person in the place to track down. I recall Easter two years ago, when I went to my house by chance, and had to recover the keys from Josefa. She was on her caretaking rounds, but the first two swimming-pooled houses I called at were most un-Spanishly chained shut. I ran her to ground in the house of an absentee Irish tycoon, and she insisted on settling me in his most expansive arm-chair, pressing on me his best brandy in a balloon glass and a cigar from his humidor, while she filled me in on village happenings. She is powerfully hospitable, but she prefers the houses in her charge to their owners, absences to presences. She scrutinizes vis-itors to our house, for she feels that they ought to suit it rather than it them. She always questions me anxiously about the house, afraid I may sell it or somehow transform it. But I can always reassure her, for over the years I have become as possessed by the sturdy quiet of the place as she is. Was I going to make a road for cars to reach the house, since I had the right to, she once asked me. I told her that I had decided instead to build a drawbridge. I think she still wonders when I am going to begin.

•

To stop at Doña Anna's store is an imperative, and its contents are as familiar to me as a working bookshelf—I can reach instinc-tively for what I need. She emerges from the gloom at the back, a bantam librarian, at any hour of the waking day. Summer, with its abundant custom, lends her benevolence; in winter she is tes-tier, knitting away the time. We have reached an arrangement over the years whereby she tots up my purchases on strips of newspaper, saving them in a drawer until just before I leave, when she sets aside an evening to add them all up, again and again, touching her thumb to her fingers. A pocket calculator would change her life, in every sense; but the luxury of not carrying money is worth the stumbling of her fingers and thumb, however much it may cost me—or her.

•

Another imperative of arriving is to track down Gonzalo, the mailman. I cannot think of anybody less suited to his vocation than Gonzalo. He dislikes the printed word, in the first place, and when he receives the mail he glares at it, letter by letter. The mail of foreigners sends him close to frenzy, and he so resents their confident expectation that *he* will take their mail to *them* that a small knot of the less trusting cluster around his door at mail time, stoking his irritability. Catch him at work in a garden and he is wryly amiable; but catch him in his cramped office or on his erratic round and he is a surly beast, an anti-mailman. Stories about him abound—mail in trees, old mail secreted in a trunk under his bed, his private hoard of postcards—but the villagers are mostly used to him and have found their own ways of prizing their mail loose from him. He has never delivered mail to me, for the house is the farthest outpost of inhabited land, and his bike could not climb to the ridge. But some years ago I took him a metal spring clip with my son's name, my own, and the name of the house pasted to it, and hung it on a nail in his office. He beamed with delight, as though I had invented the wheel, and has stuck our letters in it ever since. Even so, I occasionally receive a letter that is a year old. Where it has passed the interim, only Gonzalo knows.

•

In the village, all roads lead to Don Anselmo; and eventually mine does, too, for talking to him is like talking to the village incarnate. He says what it would say. None of the villagers would think of taking a job, selling land, or making a will without first seeking him out on the terrace of his *pensión* and listening to his wise, unobtrusive opinion. His kindness is just as unostentatious, yet almost everyone in the village has been touched by it, often in practical form. He serves as the conscience of the place and has managed to stave off some of the more extravagant follies of foreigners by being the sort of presence it would be painful to offend. (I have seen him occasionally mutter into his soup, however, at the mention of some name or other, and he turns a dangerous color at any reference to one settler, who, out of well-heeled boredom, compulsively builds rustic extensions to her already overlarge domain, paradoxically compounding her solitude.) The past unreels easily from his prodigious memory, for he is a walking chronicle of the place, and from his terrace he will point out a house and supply the history of its inhabitants, anecdote by anecdote. Lately the village's declining population has made him disconsolate; but while ruefully lamenting its death he is forever coming up with schemes to bring the place back to life.

I find him surrounded by newspapers on his terrace, overlooking the lower village from his armchair with the concern of a lifeguard, pointing out small appearances—dogs, mules, people. "Can you remember now when you came here first?" he asks me. "Antonio still baked our bread every day, we butchered our own sheep, there was plenty of work, with the charcoal-burning, there was coming and going in the café, the carts left before dawn every day for the market, there were only two cars besides the bus, we used to barter our vegetables and pay our bills annually. Now, I know that when anybody begins to talk like this, it is a sign of growing old. But I have not lost my wits. I'm not talking about the kind of nostalgia that foreigners have, looking for forgotten villages and handmade existences. You know very well how that often infuriates us, for these things smack of a time when Spaniards had little enough to eat, when our hands were all we had. I *know* that plastic bags are uglier than baskets, but I know, too, that our lives are a lot more abundant than they were when we had to work all the waking day. I won't go over the Franco years. I'm ashamed of that time—that we let it happen. A country without politics is a dead country. I am being neither sentimental nor romantic; it's just that I look back again and again to a time when this village had an equilibrium of its own, which we saw going on and on. We worked hard, we delivered our own children and buried our own dead, we didn't need help from the outside, the place was fruitful. I know in my bones it was a good time, and it pains me to think it has probably gone forever. We had village politics, but we were small enough for them to remain human politics. We didn't need to belong to parties. We are too remote to make much difference to the new Spain—or, rather, it won't make much difference to us. Now, I have been thinking, and I need your help." I wondered what was coming, for there was a visionary gleam in Don Anselmo's eye. "There must be a number of villages in Europe, perhaps some in your country, where they have the opposite problem from us—plenty of hands and no work. If we could only get in touch with one of these, we could make an arrangement where they sent us down six or eight strong men for the summer. We could easily house them here and pay them a little—perhaps they'd enjoy coming to work in the sun, and my wife could teach them Spanish. We shall write a letter to several newspapers, and you can help me to translate it. I should have thought of it years ago. I'm sure that if we get all the fallow land planted, those who have left will think of coming back." As Joaquín the mason always says, Don Anselmo should be in Madrid. They need him there.

•

Although I know only a few of the foreigners who live in the place—there are supposed to be twenty-seven, but no one seems in a position to make an accurate count, since one or two have apparently not been seen for years—I know the nicknames of a good many of them. The villagers never attempt to pronounce foreign names but have a collective genius for fastening identifying nicknames to the strangers in their midst—and, indeed, they do it to one another, too. The nicknames have a knack of settling on the most distinguishing characteristics: a Dutchman who remains here to nurse his alcoholism is known as Señor Sacacorchos, Mr. Corkscrew, and actually has a corkscrew look; a finicky Englishman with the habit of checking all his pencilled bills for errors is called El Matemático, the Mathematician; a German who is wont to talk to imaginary animals is known as El Ventrílocuo; a Venezuelan violinist and his blonde, parrot-tempered wife are always referred to together as Los Demoledores, the Wreckers, so often does the sound of breaking glass and furniture resound from their enraged house. But who is the one they call La Sudadora, She Who Sweats? And will I be able to recognize La Manoteadora, She Who Waves Her Hands, in a place where everyone does? I'm sure I will. Not many know their own nicknames, for the system is so arranged as to give the impression to everyone that he is the nicknameless exception. I know mine through the accident of coming down behind Gonzalo's house one afternoon while he was trying to identify the recipient of an overseas letter as his wife ran through the whole cast of nicknames before my ears. But, for luck's sake, I would no more reveal it than I would leave nail clippings or hair trimmings lying about.

•

One afternoon, I come on Ignacio painting the tailgate of his truck in a rage. He gesticulates at me, spraying black paint. "Three weeks ago, they painted 'AMNISTÍA' on the truck, and that was fine. I felt quite good with it there. But last night I had to park the truck in town for the early market, and this morning someone had painted 'FRANCO' on my tail. Now, that's too much. Besides, people will begin to think I'm a turncoat."

He lays his brush down carefully. "I remember, during the Republic, we'd sometimes hear noises at night, and in the morning we'd find the whole street wall of the house plastered with posters. Not so many people in the villages knew how to read and write then, so the parties would print these picture posters with a slogan on them and slap them up in villages through the night with cheap paste. If they weren't of our party, we'd wash them

171

off in the morning. But what about now, when we've got literacy, and spray paint, and armfuls of new parties, and a country full of blank walls? I hope they mean what they write, because it will never come off." He waves his arm dramatically across the façades of the descending houses, and I am suddenly aware of how many expanses of pristine white wall there are. "Take a last look at all the white walls of Spain!"

•

The market town, the provincial capital, is only some twenty miles from us, but I take my cue from Doña Isabel and Doña Matilde, who have never gone there in their lives. In the village, although meat is sparse and the chickens are muscular, fruit and vegetables abound. Besides, I have no machines to break down, nor a car needing gasoline. Town occasions do crop up, however—tickets to be booked, a friend to be met, banks to be visited close to bill-paying time. I make the journey reluctantly, for it means wearing clothes and shoes and putting on a civilized face. The bus leaves before the sun has touched the village, and we reach the town when it is scarcely awake. Shopgirls are watering their stretches of sidewalk, and two men are drinking *aguardiente* in a café to fuel their morning. The town was once an agreeable and quite graceful provincial capital, with bookbinders and bucket menders in its back streets, trams, and a fleet of vintage taxis, some of them running on gas given off by almond husks, which smoldered over a charcoal brazier attached to the back of the cab. The tourist boom of the sixties, however, grafted on top of it the trappings of a city—tourist and airline offices, sleek banks, Formica cafés, and, of course, automobiles, which have turned the place into a misery of congestion. One or two cafés stay the same, the waiters familiar as uncles. There used to be a celebrated waiter who served drinks in a bar and dinner in a nearby restaurant simultaneously, flitting back and forth on a bicycle.

I go to the bank—an ordeal that in Spain is a kind of office theatre. You are given a paper number, and your check, with an identical number pinned to it, is dropped in some abandoned "in" tray, the proprietor of which is deep in conversation or a newspaper. By the time your number is called, you know all the bank employees well enough by sight to nod at them instinctively in the street. I make a sally into the market. Its variety is blinding after the village—especially that of the fish market, outside which an army of cats paces expectantly. Several times, I cross the path of Ignacio, and we greet each other like survivors. He brings his truck down on weekdays to stock Doña Anna's store, but at the same time he carries a list of bizarre commissions: thread for Doña Matilde, a well pulley, whitewash, flypaper, eccentric electrical fittings—for the village technology is long out of date, and replacements can now be found only in dusty stores in back streets, which he alone knows. My last stop is to buy newspapers and magazines, and, with these, I arrive in relief at the café we use as our outpost in town. It is run by a man from the village, and in our eyes it has the status of an embassy—we leave messages and baskets there, and seek asylum until bus time. Don Anselmo spends Saturday mornings there, and those who have moved to town from the village still come to ask his counsel. Sebastián, the bus driver, is a pillar of the place and glows with importance; for when he leaves, we leave. We do eventually and gratefully.

•

One day, the sound of the bell floats up from the church. We stop talking. It goes on tolling. We stand still and listen to it. In a small place of around a hundred souls, which is what we number in summer, a death reverberates. Who has died? Antonio, the retired baker, who reads only old newspapers and so is always full of strange news? Consuelo, who used to sell us chickens, all of which she knew by name? The old people inhabit a continuum in the village. They are its most permanent fixtures, they are honored and listened to, and their absence remains tangible. When we go down later in the day, people are standing about in twos

173

and threes, talking. Consuelo, on her terrace, is wearing a black shawl. It is Doña Esperanza, of the high orchard, who has died, after being ill for more than a year. I remember her as someone wrapped in sadness. Doña Anna has closed her store. The whole village has stopped. Joaquín the mason, Doña Esperanza's nephew, is sitting on the wall outside the café, strange and grave in suit and tie. Inside, Don Anselmo silently hands a glass of brandy to everyone who enters. There is not much conversation. The whole village will attend the funeral; and until it is over we will all think about death. There will be much headshaking and much spoiling of the children.

•

I do not own a watch and pass the summer without ever knowing the time. There is nothing to know it for, except the morning bus. Doña Anna's store is her house, and so is always open except for periods of sleep. Now and then, if the air is still enough, I can hear the chimes from the church clock wavering up to us, but never distinctly enough to count them. We have a crude measure of our own, however. As the sun rises, it projects through the top window and onto the white back wall a rectangle of orange light, which yellows and descends in the course of the morning. Thanks to a visiting watch, we have marked a crude scale on the wall— the first touch of light is approaching six o'clock, the top of the picture is nine, its bottom edge ten. It serves for the summer. I think I have twice missed the bus, but that may not have been the sun's fault, for Sebastián, unless he is forewarned, is apt to leave on whim, as long as there is at least one passenger for conversation. He, too, is watchless. And the church clock, bought by subscription six years ago, often veers ten minutes in either direction from the correct time, they tell me. But how do they know?

•

One morning early, as I am peeling fruit in the kitchen, an explosion of sound engulfs the house. I rush to the terrace, too late to see the plane; but another is following, directly over us, only a hundred meters up—a light plane with Spanish Air Force markings. We hear them circling over the far side of the valley, then droning back seaward, to return some half hour later, diving down on us and swishing the trees. What have we done? Planes never cross our sky. Then, as the planes are making their third run, Eugenio appears, to say that the far side of the mountain has been burning since early morning and that the planes are dropping chemicals. The house is an obvious landmark for them. That evening, the mountain is haloed from behind in red. But the planes do not come back, and the fire burns out. All summer, we hear and read of drought and fires. Near the River Ebro, the newspapers tell us, brushfires have been exploding shells buried since the Civil War. Then, late in August, after a brooding morning, the skies tear and rain obliterates us, lacerating the terrace. I wait until the roof is washed off, then connect the gutter pipe to the well entry. The deep boom of the water gushing in does wonders for our spirits and eventually sends us to sleep in satisfaction. Next morning, the summer, wiped clean of fire and water, is blue and clear and permanent again.

•

I cannot remember at the moment the details of closing the house and leaving, except that I know I forgot to untie the clothesline. When I think of the house now, I think not of the summer past but of all summers in one, of sitting on the terrace under a crowded night sky, layered in biological time. And yet, at will, I can remember the contents of a miscellaneous drawer—green glass marbles, a pack of Spanish playing cards with *copas* and *bastos*, a dolphin pendant left behind, a stop sign that we used to hang on the first tree on the path, electric bills, shopping lists in various languages, the house keys. The house serves me as an extra vantage point, from which I can take a different fix on existence. It also gives me a commitment to Spain. I telephone summer friends I made in the village, but we are separated by other lives, the village no more than a small territory in common. The photographs have been developed, wax effigies of August, but they are less substantial than the image of the village in my head. Indeed, on my first few evenings back in the world, I open my front door and half expect to find, instead of a groomed London square, the pale shape of the mountain under the moon, the still almond trees, and the stone terrace we once laid by hand.

•

Summer 1981

To live in the village, even temporarily, is to translate existence into a pure particularity. The silence is primordial, and the only sounds that violate it are those that I make myself. I grow more respectful of the natural world, and feel my presence as something of an intrusion. But I think of being there less as an escape than as a corrective; it gives me time to put my priorities in order. Although Spain has loomed large in my life, my specific attachment is to the village—to the children I have seen grow up and to the villagers I have watched grow old. However much one learns about and understands a country in terms of events, it is the lived experience that matters most, and I looked forward keenly to picking up the long, unfinished conversations, the view from the inside.

•

There is a sense in which all Spanish villages are interchangeable: they have in common a manner of being, a vantage point, and, in this present Spain, a plight. Having lived in four separate villages, I think I would feel at ease in any—in its rituals and hierarchies, in its dingy, loquacious café, in its human rhythm. Spanish villages bear to each other family likenesses. It is only when

NOTES FROM A SPANISH VILLAGE

one gets to know a village by name—landscape, houses, people—
that it becomes a quite separate drama, a web of connections and
commitments, even of argument. Not that our village is ever rent
by civic strife—it has waned considerably from its self-sustaining, self-regulating days, and is now administered bureaucrati-
cally from the anonymous outside as part of the region. Still, it
generated its own garbage collection ahead of other villages, and
the forces of law and order have had no cause to visit since local
traffic in contraband stopped, except for one occasion, when a
drink-crazed Norwegian ecologist let the air out of the tires on
the twenty-odd cars in the place, walking about four mountainous miles to do it.

•

When I first land in Spain now, I find it hard to recall the grayness
of the Franco years, the years of restraint. Now the kiosks blaze
with newspapers and magazines, the stores abound, the police
seem less forbidding. There is a general jauntiness, an exuberance,
in the streets. I haggle with a taxi-driver, and soon we have left
the town behind and are climbing through the olive groves, the
earth reddened by the evening sun. The lower houses straggle
into sight, and then the church spire, the appearance of the place
confirming memory yet still carrying the pleasure of discovery.
The taxi whines up through the village to the highest point and
leaves me off on the ridge, the village now below me and the
house a short, stumbling walk away. As the sound of the taxi
wanes, the huge silence descends. The key is there under the
stone, and as I turn it in the lock and shoulder the door open a
whole dormant identity settles upon me—a self I have left there,
like the old work coat hanging on its wooden peg. I spend some
time pacing the place, opening drawers, fingering objects, noticing. During my absence, various friends have been to stay and
have left traces—an abandoned ticket, a new kitchen knife, odd
books, a drawing tacked to the wall. I go out on the terrace in the
afterglow, drop the bucket in the well, and draw it up brim-

ming—a ritual act. Everything here has to be done by hand, which makes the head more attentive. In that silence, other worlds recede, the mail their only manifestation.

•

The first morning is always a revelation, the surprise of waking up into another place, another self. My eyes go round the room, surprised by familiar objects—the jasper stone in its niche in the white wall, the oak chest from the flea market, books, candlesticks, pictures, the icons of the house. Then, bare feet on the tile floor, a step out to the stone terrace, the gasp of early morning. The sun is barely over the mountain's shoulder and is just beginning to warm. The vine has been cut back to light green beginnings, the passionflowers, trained round the door, are beginning to open, and I begin to notice everywhere the hand of Eugenio. I open the well and draw a bucket of the water left by the winter rain, the rattle of the chain and the clank of the bucket like a tune I know well. I spend the next hour prowling about the house, picking up objects, touching books, in a kind of greeting. On the desk upstairs Josefa has left one wild orchid in a glass—a lucky flower, she always tells me, for it appears unpredictably in the forest and can only be found, not looked for. I unpack, and already the things in my bag look alien, from another world. I find some work clothes in a drawer and put them on. It is like putting on the place again, regaining a lost self. I am here.

•

To a village as small as ours, rituals are essential, and I go down the path in late morning to enact the rituals of arrival—the gnarled handshakes, the embraces, and the formal exchanges that might be scripted in stone. There is much headshaking and hand-wringing, accompanied by the gnomic sentences that seem so indigenous to the Spanish language, the natural proverbs that crop up in village conversations. Later on, I gather, bit by bit, all that has gone on in my absence, in many differing versions, variously edited by the tellers, and I put together the missing time, which is difficult, for the people here do not talk in years but in seasons, enumeration by weather and fruits and harvests. I listen a lot at first, and the happenings emerge—a forest fire, a death, a family feud—to fill in the gap in my time. It has been a winter of wind; but without much rain—alas, for the *cisternas* in the village are filled from the guttered roofs, and the supply of summer water depends on the ferocity of the winter rains. From May on, however, we do not talk of the weather, for it is steadily blue and hot and dry, with only infinitesimal variations. In summer, village life shifts down to half speed. Time stretches, people walk more slowly, everything moves in a sunstruck drift. May, however, has its surprises. I woke one morning early, to seemingly less light, and went out on the terrace to find myself in an eerie cold grayness. A cloud had settled on our small mountain, and I was standing in the middle of it, barely able to see the nearest almond tree. In under an hour, the sun had burned it away, but even in that short time I felt that I had been in and out of a separate season.

•

Nowadays the village abounds in cars, parked precariously outside the remote houses. Now a number of its inhabitants drive to work every day in the market town some thirty kilometers away. The empty houses have been bought up, not by foreigners but by Spaniards prosperous enough to afford a weekend retreat, and they open up and resound from Friday until Monday, the property of strangers who use the place without any pretense of belonging, leaving the remaining inhabitants to man it like a skeleton crew. A number of the foreigners who lived here permanently have drifted off to their homelands; now the old ones form more than half of the population, and it gives the place a certain mournful note, for they are the last survivors of a rural Spanish past, and with them goes the village's onetime equilibrium. The once fruitful land surrounding the village dies with them. Between them and the grandchildren they helped to raise exists an enormous gulf, the gulf between that rustic self-sufficiency and the technological present. The grandchildren come back in their cars to visit them occasionally, from a world that has left them behind. The new Spain is beyond them. They have become spectators rather than participants, and I often catch an expression of wary sadness crossing their weathered faces.

•

I drop in at Josefa's house, to confirm my presence. She crows with satisfaction, and sits me down in her kitchen while she chronicles the missing time for me. A large, handsome woman, she is for me the incarnation of the place. Behind her recounting of everyday events is an awe of life and death, a sense of the transitory nature of everything, which leads her, perversely, to give the living present her vivid attention. The village is her world, known to her by name and sight, so that when I leave the place I feel that for her I cease to exist; conversely, when I arrive she looks on me like Lazarus and busies herself with telling me what I have missed, as though there were no real life outside the perimeter of the village. Her greeting is always the same—her wide smile, her flare of vivacity, and "*Mira! Sobrevivimos!*" (Look! We have survived!). This time, I am as amazed as she is. A portrait of Josefa by a passing French painter hangs in the place of honor in her living room, and she has a drawerful of photographs of herself taken by people whose houses she has cared for. "It was I who should have taken pictures of them," she tells me, laughing.

•

The entire village turned out for the general election of June 1977. Josefa never tires of talking about it. Although she is in her sixties, it was her first experience of voting, for the last free general election in Spain had taken place in 1936. She stayed around the schoolhouse where the voting took place most of the day, consumed by curiosity over how her neighbors voted, and brought soup with her for other enthusiasts. The only drawback she finds in the democratic system, she tells me, is the long interval between elections. She would like them to be held every month and is already planning her next campaign.

•

In the world of the village, death is a reduction, and among the old ones its inevitability sits like an attendant bird, like imminent nightfall. I feel the reduction more on this occasion, for during my absence Don Anselmo has died. His absence is almost as tangible as his presence, for it was he, more than anyone else, who gave the place a direction and a human shape. He had been mayor, as had his father, and he carried the annals of the place in his head, its past as vivid to him as its present. From his huge, worn armchair in the little *pensión* that he ran and where he was always to be found, he dispensed advice, stories, help, and unflagging kindness—something like a tribal headman, with a patient ear and an inexhaustible generosity of spirit. He had become so identified with the place that its well-being mattered more to him than his own, and I could not help feeling that with his death the spirit had gone out of it. I would often call on him in the late afternoon, and on this occasion, when that time of day came around, I felt at loose ends, I felt the deprivation of his death. One afternoon, I went down and collected the key to the small cemetery from the bar under the priest's house. I sat under a cypress tree, remembering an afternoon with Don Anselmo in that same spot, where he had told me about the other occupants of the sandstone niches, bringing them to life one by one. His own niche bears only his name and the legend *"Primera Y Última Morada,"* first and last resting place. For Spaniards, death is neither a surprise nor a puzzle, since they invoke it so often in their daily conversation. As they approach it, they make of it a familiar, a silent companion to whom they look more and more. I find it easy, sitting here, to imagine Don Anselmo back into being, to play back a conversation with him, to hear his solemn voice recounting some part of the long narrative of the village. Now that he is dead, it is as though the place had suddenly lost its memory, as though all its annals lie there encased in stone, unreadable now, fading, buried.

•

It was during the sixties that I saw most of Don Anselmo. His wife knew both French and English and was an inveterate reader of magazines, which she summarized for Don Anselmo. It was thus that he became passionately interested in ecology, for he discovered that he had been its unwitting champion all his life. I once gave him a copy of *The Whole Earth Catalog*, and it was never far from his armchair. What excited him was the discovery that agricultural self-sufficiency and village-size communities were constantly invoked as ecological ideals, and he began more than ever to feel that the village of yesteryear had been something of an ecological Eden, if a threadbare one. Gravely, he began to advance schemes by which the village might give a further lead to the rest of the world. He tried to ban cars from the place, but since the old people depended on the bus, he relented. Our air, besides, is milk and honey. He proposed advertising for hippies to come and make fertile lately abandoned land, but he was dissuaded by some horrified foreign inhabitants. He considered bringing back the bartering of crops and goods, a ritual over which he had once presided, but since the only commodity that certain inhabitants could produce was money, he was again defeated by circumstance. He was always trying to think up small, productive enterprises for people in the village, but he could not prevent the drift toward the town, where the pickings were more immediate. In his later years, when the village ceased to be a working place and instead lived well enough off the leisure of others, a sadness grew about him, for his ideal had almost existed and, ironically, had been eroded by progress. Almost the last time I saw him, his conversation caused me to feel that he had given up and had equated the death of the village with his own. I remember well what he said. "I have decided that what those learned people tell us about how we are using up the world, how we must live in harmony with what we have, has come too late for us. Perhaps it *could* have happened if we had heeded, but I do not think that it will happen now. Yet here we once lived just like that, although we no longer do. That pains me—I find myself thinking more and more of those days, and wishing them back." Some eight months later, I had a letter from my son, who was there at the time, telling me of Don Anselmo's death, and of his funeral, which brought out the whole population, and many from the region, in mourning for his huge lost presence and for the past he took with him. We do not stop at the *pensión* now, as we once did. As Eugenio once said, out of the air, "I cannot bear to look at that empty armchair. It is too big for any of us."

•

The great fiestas of summer—Corpus Christi, San Juan—shut down Spain like a muffling Sunday, but they do not much affect the village, for we have almost nothing to shut down, nothing to suspend. The one day in the summer of 1981 that brought the place to holiday attention was the royal wedding of Prince Charles to Lady Diana Spencer, which Spanish television carried in all its prolonged pageantry. In the days preceding the event, however, the picturesque surface had been ruffled by the announcement that the royal couple would fly on their honeymoon to Gibraltar, where they would board the royal yacht *Britannia.* That announcement stopped Spain in its tracks, for the question of Gibraltar is one that has plagued relations between Spain and England ever since the British assumed sovereignty over the Rock in 1704. Consternation at the decision dominated the newspapers, and a reaction was not slow in coming, for the following day King Juan Carlos announced that he and Queen Sofía would not be attending the wedding in London as planned. Spanish heads nodded vehement approval: Had the British government been stupid enough not to realize what the stopover might imply, or arrogant enough to brush it aside? Or was the landing in Gibraltar intended as a deliberate slight to Spain, as some of the more cynical commentators suggested? On and off ever since 1704, Gibraltar has been a vexing bone of contention between the two countries, and the arguments over it have created a mass of papers and documents that by now must rival the Rock itself in bulk.

In any case, the wedding itself had been given wide attention in the press, and since it meant one day of morning television— still a novelty in Spain—the promise of spectacle triumphed over national indignation, and the country turned its attention to the event. I let my curiosity lead me down to the village in midmorning, for all the public television sets were sure to be turned on. There was a choice. In the *pensión*, chairs had been arranged in rows, and the fat color set—twice the size of its small black-and-white ancestor—had been dusted and crested with flowers. By the time I got there, however, the seats had all been taken, mostly by the resident foreign population, the British contingent dominant as self-appointed translators and explainers to the others. Manolo was behind the bar, helping out and paying little notice to the unrolling pomp. He shrugged at me, and I understood. I did not linger there but went up to the *estanco*, where we buy our stamps and tobacco, and which gives houseroom to an even bigger set, in the back of the store. The place was already taken over, however, mostly by children, who were bent on turning the day into a romp, so I left and went farther up the road, to Doña Anna's store, which had a small, enfeebled black-and-white set in the back, but more discriminating patrons, I hoped. They were already bent over the screen in the dimness of the back room, peering, and with them sat Fulgencio, who had been delivering melons from the next village. Fulgencio is our local Socialist, adamant and serious, and we had hardly shaken hands before he was gesturing indignantly at the screen.

I pulled up a chair beside Doña Anna, who was full of questions. "Are these people Catholics?" she asked me abruptly, jerking her head at the interior of St. Paul's Cathedral. I attempted to run through the history of the Reformation for her in potted form, and she did a lot of headshaking. "It looks just like my little niece Margarita's wedding last year—I can't see the difference," she said. The Spanish announcer was full of background information and statistics, quite a lot of the data in the form of financial assessment, which Fulgencio whistled over. I have noticed that Spaniards like to talk about large sums of money, as though luxuriating in their immensity, and when the announcer informed us that the wedding was costing well over a hundred million pesetas Doña Anna crossed herself at once, and Fulgencio whistled and rolled his eyes upward. It was more than the annual stipend that King Juan Carlos drew, he informed us importantly. He muttered at everything. Did I think that Juan Carlos had been right not to attend the wedding, he asked me suddenly, and when I told him that I did he looked nonplussed for a moment. Doña Anna poured us all a glass of wine. The Spanish announcer, meanwhile, was translating the text of a hymn being sung by loyal subjects—quite deftly, I thought, although he had just previously confessed himself bewildered by some of the more remote branches of the British royal-family tree. The ceremony concluded; Fulgencio relaxed. As we watched the jubilant crowds in the streets, he leaned over to me confidingly. "I have to tell you that the English puzzle me more than anybody alive," he said. "They appear so civilized, so intelligent, and yet are so stupid. That Prince Charles—would he ever be able to speak to his people the way Juan Carlos spoke to us last February? Not twelve days ago, I was watching films of young English people rioting in the streets, pelting the police with bottles and bricks—the same police they are dancing with at this very moment. Does that make sense? Are we as incomprehensible to them as they are to us?" There was no possible answer, and Fulgencio said his good-byes and left.

Doña Anna sighed and shook her head. I rose to go, too, and she came with me to the door. "What I don't understand," she told me, "is that they should spend all that money and ceremony on a wedding when they will probably separate, the way all foreigners do." I tried to reassure her. Poor Doña Anna. Most of the foreigners who have lived in the village at different times have indeed separated and regrouped, to her great consternation, and village monogamy has become to her something of a citadel, assailed by the outside world.

·

From my first visit on, simply being in Spain has always occasioned in me a kind of joy, a physical tingle, which comes from a whole crop of elements: its light, its landscape, its language, and most of all its human rhythm, a manner of being that graces the place. It comes, however, not from any such abstract awareness but from intense particularities: bare village cafés loud with argument and dominoes, or else sleepy and empty except for flies; sudden memorable conversations with strangers; the way Spaniards have of imposing human time, so that meals and meetings last as long as they need to. There is a durability about the Spanish people, an acceptance of fate that, paradoxically, gives them a keen sense of the present, a gleeful spontaneity. Their own eccentricities make them tolerant of the oddness of others, which helped them to survive the descent of the tourist hordes. Spain has a sparse, bare, uncluttered look, from its empty landscapes to its stark interiors. Time spent in the village always serves to unencumber me, to a point where the days seem wondrously long, gifts of time, where the weather simplifies existence to a vocabulary of elemental acts, like drawing water or making fire, where a visit to the village store is the only necessity. The current of village life does not alter, even though its population has shrivelled. It has a few ritual points—Don Anselmo's *pensión*, Doña Anna's store, the church, Gonzalo's patio at mail time, the daily bus to the market town—but otherwise it keeps to itself. So it has been insulated from most of the changes taking place in urban Spain, at least until very recently. Perhaps it is the cumulation of the last few decades of lack, to say nothing of the preceding centuries', that has lent such gusto to the consuming mania that grips Spain at the moment, a craving for comfort after those bleak, wooden years. One day, Joaquín the mason, who has come to fix a leak in the roof gutter, talks to me about the "Híper" (he says "eee-pair," as though it were a spell), the new wonder of the region. He is going, the next day, to buy a drill, and he will take me, he promises. I meet him at his car, which he had acquired only a few months before and has just learned to drive, though he is a veteran of the Civil War. He crawls along, muttering to himself. The car is an enemy. The Hípermercado turns out to be a building as large as an airplane hangar, with racks of goods that disappear into a gaudy distance, bearing everything from Rioja wines and sides of beef to four-poster beds and outboard motors. Spanish families come for a whole Sunday to gawk, to eat and drink, and inevitably to buy. Joaquín finds his drill, and, sensing his unease, I tell him I'd as soon leave, though not before I have bought four bottles of Marqués de Riscal wine. Joaquín tells me on the way home that he took his family some weeks ago—disastrously, for his grandson grew tearfully attached to a tractor-type lawnmower and would not be prized from it, while his wife and daughter were irresistibly drawn to dresses and gadgets. He has forbidden a return visit, he says grimly. I doubt if he will tell them where he bought his drill.

•

Whatever Franco thought his legacy to Spain would be, he cannot have imagined that it would be a kind of deliberate oblivion. Spain's reaction to the Franco years has been to remove them abruptly to a remote past, to see them over all as a limbo. He still turns up on an occasional stamp or coin, but these effigies are numbered. I recall seeing, a couple of years ago, in a boutique in Barcelona, a desk legend that read "FRANCO STILL DEAD!" Now no such confirmation is necessary; he does not haunt the feast. The older ones are still wondering to themselves how they could have let him last so long. The younger generations feel as though they had been released from prison after a false arrest. The living present has obliterated that past in the manner of a windshield wiper. The Spanish novelist Juan Goytisolo, who lived in self-imposed exile during the Franco years, wrote a searing essay on him soon after his death, a painful summation of the years lived in his pervasive shadow:

> Hangman and at the same time involuntary creator of modern Spain—it is up to the historians, and not to me, to clarify exactly what he did over the last forty years, avoiding both the distortions of official hagiography and the deformations of his black reputation.
>
> At the time of his death, I would prefer to dwell on what his existence has meant for us who were children during the Civil War—men and women who today are condemned to the anomalous situation of growing old without having known, because of him, either youth or responsibility. Perhaps the distinctive characteristic of the era we had to live through has been just that: the impossibility of our realizing a free and mature life of action, of influencing in any way the fate of our society outside of the ways laid down once and for all by him, with the necessary consequence of reducing every individual's sphere of action to his private life, or forcing him into an egocentric struggle for his personal survival, under the law of force. . . . Besides the censorship sustained by him, his regime created something worse: the habit of self-censorship and spiritual atrophy that has condemned Spaniards to practice the elusive art of reading between the lines, of having always to present a censor with the monstrous power of wounding them. . . . [His regime created] an enormous mass of citizens doomed to be in a perpetual legal minority: no right to vote, to buy a newspaper with opinions differing from those of the government, to read a book or see a movie that was not censored, to associate with other unconforming citizens, to protect against abuses, to organize into unions. . . . A people that has lived

almost forty years in conditions of irresponsibility and im-
potence is a people necessarily sick, whose convalescence
may last as long as the illness did. . . .

His fierce attachment to life—that obstinate durability
which so surprised those attending his endless death agony—throws an even blacker light on the figure who, a few
weeks before, coldly condemned to death, without taking
any account of worldwide protest, five young compatriots,
guilty of the unpardonable sin of replying with violence to
the legalized violence of his government.

It costs me dear, but I force my lips to say it, on the clear
condition that he does not go on ruling from his tomb: inasmuch as Spain, freed at last from his presence, lives and
breathes again, may he rest in peace.

Spain's convalescence proved much shorter than Goytisolo
feared. Spaniards, with that ruthlessness that I have glimpsed in
them at odd moments, devised for Franco the ultimate revenge—
not simply forgetting him but acting now as though he had never
existed.

•

I have spent many days, in different years and seasons, alone in
the house, as I am now, the silence huge and unbroken except by
my own noises, by occasional birds and sheep bells, and sometimes by the fluting sound of children singing from the pine-
woods across from the house, children from the summer retreat,
out walking with an accompanying nun. Nobody comes, except
by intention. Eugenio appears at odd times, to attend to the trees
or to do the accounts. The almond crop is poor, he says—it was
a winter of wind, not enough rain. I help him carry fertilizer
down to the lower terrace, and then spend an hour or two clearing
brush in the ilex forest behind the house. A cuckoo makes its slow
way up the valley, loudmouthed against the quiet. I sit on the
terrace and gaze. The edge of roof shadow is suddenly a foot

closer to my chair. It is something I have always noticed about Spaniards—how so many of them sit in their own silence as though it were a bubble enclosing them, oblivious, wholly absorbed. Gerald Brenan writes about them, "As they sit at their tables outside the cafés, their eyes record as on a photographic plate the people who are passing, but on a deeper level they are listening to themselves living." It is something I absorb from the house, which seems to impose a silence of its own. I often think of it when I am far away from it: standing stony and empty, its eyes shuttered. I read, cook, draw water, write, gather wood, not according to plan but as these things occur to me, and from time to time I wander up through the forest, to lose myself, or to watch the late sun on the mountain across from it, changing the colors on its face, etching its shadows sharply. Music tinkles away below me in the neighboring village, for they have there the beginnings of a rural disco. I walk slowly back through the ruins of the seven houses below ours, all that is left of the working hamlet it once was. Don Anselmo remembers it—remembered it. Now summer vegetation claws at the stones, and only our presence keeps it from taking over our house and similarly levelling it. It is natural, at the house, to think like a castaway, and it makes for stark thought.

•

Already, in September, the village has begun to feel like a house with too many rooms. While I am paying bills, I feel I am somehow betraying the place by going. I catch up with Eugenio on the path, and he upbraids me, as usual. "Almost a hundred kilos of grapes, which you won't even taste," he says. "You could be living well here. But if you have to go, send me somebody with a strong back who'll give me three hours' work a day. That's all I need. I get enough out of the crop and the sheep now to keep Josefa and me well enough, but if I had help we'd all be well off. Surely somebody must want to come here." We stop at the ridge to get our breath. It looks so green and golden in the afterglow of sun that I feel at that moment that almost anyone would want to come. Eugenio is rolling a cigarette. He will probably have voted again by the time I see him again, I remind him. He looks rueful. "I'd vote for Franco's grandchildren if I thought they'd give some attention to the land. As it is, I'll have to see what they come up with—the parties. I hope there's at least one sensible enough to send me some help. I may be simple, but growing food seems to me such a fundamental thing to do that I can't see why it isn't in the front of everybody's mind. It's far beyond politics. But do not forget to send me those seeds. They will be up by the time you come." We shake hands, and I tell him I hope he lives a hundred years.

•

Some of the foreigners who have come to rest in the village tell elaborate stories, carefully edited and well rubbed in the telling, of how they first stumbled on the place and forgot to leave. As my time here runs out, I think that they are not so farfetched, for the urgencies I have created for myself elsewhere seem trivial by now, and the timelessness I have grown into is something too rich to leave cursorily. But the day comes closer, inexorable as the shadow on the terrace, and I find myself looking at stones and trees as though for the last time, trying to fix the atmosphere of an afternoon like a print on my memory. Yet it is already imprinted there, from countless seasons and occasions, so completely that I can return to it in my head, in piercing detail. I know the stones marking the path as distinctly as faces, and a good number of the trees. I can summon up any time of day—the haze of early morning, the limpid, brilliant blue of noon, the ochre light following sunset that honeys the white wall. I can turn on the seasons—the drumming of the great rains, the white astonishment of the almond blossom in February, the pacific drowse of summer. I prowl through the house at will, fingering the talismans on the shelves and playing back sounds, footsteps on the path, the thud of fruit falling, the rattle of the bucket in the well.

Most of all, I can in time induce the silence of the place, as an easement of mind. I suppose it has become for me what Gerard Manley Hopkins called an inscape, for although I can recall in like detail other places I have lived in, none have the same brilliance in my memory. I have the house and the forest in my head, out of time, and now to go back to it is only to confirm its existence. It and the village have been left behind, in a fold of time, and the new Spain might almost be another country. While it presses eagerly forward, the village looks wistfully back.

I take a last walk through the ilex forest, I pile up the newspapers in the niche by the fireplace, to yellow in their good time, I seal jars against the ants, I return to Eugenio the tools he has lent me, I prepare to close the house, as though it were a time capsule that will wait, sealed and safe, until I can open it up again. Except that, this time, I feel there is something of a difference. The house has stone walls at least two feet thick, and I have always felt that, short of a cataclysmic disaster, it would wait there, in its silence, for me to open it up again. This time, however, the hazards do not emanate from the ants, the termites, the clawing vegetation, the earthquakes, or the thunderbolts. The human world has become more precarious than the natural world, and I feel that I will owe my next return less to the obdurate, stony permanence of the house than to the restraint of our own willful humanity, which has let us survive, however precariously, until now.

•

Afterword

In 1983, I received a letter from Josefa: Eugenio had died. He had grown too tired to work, she wrote. For her, the village would not be the same. She was moving to the nearby town.

In 1984, Jasper Reid decided to turn the house into money, and sold it.

In the spring of 1985, I passed briefly through Spain and made a fleeting visit to the village, on an afternoon of mist and showers. The land lay idle and overgrown, the almond trees unpruned, the almonds unpicked. Shuttered up, the house looked forlorn under the rain. I shifted it, finally, into the mode of memory.

In Memoriam, Amada

The story "In Memoriam, Amada" has a curious genesis. I had heard it told a number of times in Spain, about the poet Juan Ramón Jiménez, but from sources both wispy and unverifiable. I decided that it should best become a "fiction," that form much loved by Latin Americans in which language takes over reality, a form they use constantly to give everyday happenings a mythic cast. To give the fiction some illusion of truth, I put it in the mouth of Judas Roquín, the Costa Rica–born writer, whose work I have often translated, and who has been, for me, the source of much inspiration.

Judas Roquín told me this story, on the veranda of his mildewed house in Cahuita. Years have passed and I may have altered some details. I cannot be sure.

In 1933, the young Brazilian poet Baltasar Melo published a book of poems, *Brasil Encarnado*, which stirred up such an outrage that Melo, forewarned by powerful friends, chose to flee the country. The poems were extravagant, unbridled even, in their manner, and applied a running sexual metaphor to Brazilian life; but it was one section, "Perversions," in which Melo characterized three prominent public figures as sexual grotesques, that made his exile inevitable. Friends hid him until he could board a freighter from Recife, under cover of darkness and an assumed name, bound for Panama. With the ample royalties from his book, he was able to buy an *estancia* on the Caribbean coast of Costa Rica, not far from where Roquín lived. The two of them met inevitably, though they did not exactly become friends.

Already vain and arrogant by nature, Melo became insufferable with success and the additional aura of notorious exile. He used his fame mainly to entice women with literary pretensions, some of them the wives of high officials. In Brazil, however, he remained something of a luminary to the young, and his flight added a certain allure to his reputation, to such a point that two young Bahian poets who worked as reporters on the newspaper *Folha da Tarde* took a leave of absence to interview him in his chosen exile. They travelled to Costa Rica mostly by bus, taking over a month to reach San José, the capital. Melo's retreat was a further day's journey, and they had to cover the last eleven kilometers on foot. Arriving at evening, they announced themselves to the housekeeper. Melo, already half-drunk, was upstairs, entertaining the daughter of a campesino, who countenanced the liaison for the sake of his fields. Melo, unfortunately, chose to be outraged, and shouted, in a voice loud enough for the waiting poets to hear, "Tell those compatriots of mine that Brazil kept my poems and rejected me. Poetic justice demands that they return home and wait there for my next book." For the two frustrated pilgrims, the journey back to Bahia was nothing short of nightmare.

•

The following autumn, a letter arrived in Cahuita for Baltasar Melo from a young Bahian girl, Amada da Bonavista, confessing shyly that her reading of *Brasil Encarnado* had altered her resolve to enter a convent, and asking for the poet's guidance. Flattered, titillated, he answered with a letter full of suggestive warmth. In response to a further letter from her, he made so bold as to ask for her likeness, and received in return the photograph of an irresistible beauty. Over the course of a whole year, their correspondence grew increasingly more erotic until, on impulse, Melo had his agent send her a steamship ticket from Bahia to Panama, where he proposed to meet her. Time passed, trying his patience; and then a letter arrived, addressed in an unfamiliar hand, from an aunt of Amada's. She had contracted meningitis and was in a critical condition. Not long after, the campesino's daughter brought another envelope with a Bahia postmark. It contained the steamship ticket, and a newspaper clipping announcing Amada's death.

We do not know if the two poets relished their intricate revenge, for they remain nameless, forgotten. But although it would be hard nowadays to track down an available copy of *Brasil Encarnado*, Baltasar Melo's name crops up in most standard anthologies of modern Brazilian poetry, represented always by the single celebrated poem, "In Memoriam: Amada," which Brazilian schoolchildren still learn by heart. I translate, inadequately of course, the first few lines:

> Body forever in bloom,
> you are the only one
> who never did decay
> go gray, wrinkle, and die
> as all warm others do.
> My life, as it wears away
> owes all its light to you . . .

When Judas had finished, I of course asked him the inevitable question: Did Baltasar Melo ever find out? Did someone tell him? Roquín got up suddenly from the hammock he was sprawled in, and looked out to the white edge of surf, just visible under the rising moon. "Ask me another time," he said. "I haven't decided yet."

Other People's Houses

Having been, for many years, an itinerant, living in an alarming number of countries and places, I am no stranger to other people's houses. I am aware of a certain disreputable cast to this admission; I can almost feel my wizened little ancestors shaking their heads and wringing their hands, for in Scotland, people tend to go from the stark stone house where they first see the light to another such fortress, where they sink roots and prepare dutifully for death, their possessions encrusted around them like barnacles. Anyone who did not seem to be following the stone script was looked on as somewhat raffish, rather like the tinkers and travelling people who sometimes passed through the village where I grew up. I would watch them leave, on foot, over the horizon, pulling their worldly belongings behind them in a handcart; and one of my earliest fantasies was to run away with them, for I felt oppressed by permanence and rootedness, and my childhood eyes strayed always to the same horizon, which promised other ways of being, a life less stony and predictable.

My errant nature was confirmed by a long time I spent at sea during the Second World War, on a series of small, cramped ships, wandering all over the Indian Ocean. Then I learned that the greatest advantage was to have as little as possible, for anything extra usually got lost or stolen, and we frequently had to shoulder our worldly goods, from ship to ship. The habit stuck—today I have next to no possessions, and I have closed the door on more houses and apartments than I can remember, leaving behind what I did not immediately need. If I had a family crest, it should read *omnia mea mecum porto* (all that is mine I carry with me); but it would get left behind.

Innocent in themselves, houses can be given quite different auras, depending on the dispositions of their occupants—they can be seen as monuments to permanence, or as temporary shelters. In Scotland, you find abundant examples of the first on the fringes of small towns, standing in well-groomed gardens, their brasses gleaming, their blinds half-drawn like lowered eyelids, domestic museums served by near-invisible slaves. When I first came to the United States, I felt it to be immediately liberating, in its fluidity, its readiness to change. Few people lived in the place they were born, moving held no terrors, and renting was the norm. Yet people inhabited their temporary shelters as though they might live there forever; and paradoxically, I felt at home. When I began to spend a part of each year in Spain, my other adopted country, I rented a series of sturdy peasant houses devoid of decoration, with whitewashed walls and tile floors, and no furnishings beyond the essentials of beds, tables, cross, and chairs. It was a time when a number of unanchored people came to rest in Spain— painters for the light, writers for the silence—setting up working outposts in the sun, whose constant presence does simplify existence. Within these anonymous white walls, one re-created one's own world—essential books and pictures, whatever other transforming elements lay to hand.

In Spain, I grew very aware of houses as presences—perhaps the residual aura of those who had lived lifetimes in them, perhaps a peculiarity of the space they enclosed. I recall visiting a house in Mallorca in the company of Robert Graves, and hearing him, after only a few minutes in the house, making peremptory excuses to leave. "Didn't you feel the bad luck in that house?" he said to me once we were out of earshot. With time, I came to feel what he meant, not in terms of good or bad luck, but of feeling welcome or unwelcome in the houses themselves, apart from the inhabitants.

Of all writers, Vladimir Nabokov read the interiors of other people's houses much as psychics read palms or tarot cards: with a wicked accuracy, he would decipher absent owners from the contents of rooms, from shelves, pictures, and paraphernalia. When he lectured at Cornell University, it was his practice, instead of having a house of his own, to rent the houses of others absent on sabbatical; and behind him already was a wandering life of exile in England, Germany, and France, in rented premises. Summers he spent in pursuit of butterflies, in motels across the United States; and when, with recognition, he came to rest, it was in a hotel apartment in Montreux, Switzerland. These various houses and interiors inhabit his books as vividly as living characters—he is always making precise connections between people and the places they choose to live in, between objects and their owners. His *Look at the Harlequins!* is a positive hymn to other people's houses.

I know just what he means. The act of inhabiting and humanizing a house, of changing it from impersonal space to private landscape, is an extremely complex one, a series of careful and cumulative choices; and, in living in other people's houses, one lives among their decisions, some inspired, others hardly thought through. I make for the bookshelves with a crow of expectation, for the books, however miscellaneous or specialized they may be, always yield up at least a handful I have never read, or even heard of, and travelling has deprived me of the possibility of keeping a library, beyond a shelf of essential or immediate reading. Kitchens are a less calculable adventure. Some of them are like shrines, where cooking has been raised to a level of high art, and invite culinary adventure; others, incomprehensibly, are as bare as hospital labs in plague-prone countries, their refrigerators bearing no more than a few viruses flourishing in jars, two or three bottles of what can only be assumed to be an antidote.

At one point in our lives, my son and I lived in London, on a houseboat we actually owned, though temporarily, moored at Cheyne Walk, in Chelsea. We had three special friends, families that lived in other parts of London; and we came to an arrangement with them to exchange houses from time to time, for appropriate weekends. We had a loose agreement—we left behind clean sheets and towels, a "reasonable amount" of food and drink, and, for the curious, some correspondence that could be read. We all relished these unlikely vacations, since we left one another elaborately written guidebooks, and we could take in another part of London—markets, greengrocers, pubs, restaurants. I often wonder why people never think of doing that oftener, except at the wrong times.

In our travels, my son and I occupied rented houses and apartments from Barcelona to Buenos Aires. He can remember every one of them in detail, down to its sounds—the creak and shudder of the houseboat as it rose off the Thames mud on the incoming tide, a house in Chile with a center patio cooled by the cooing of doves, a cottage in Scotland in a wood of its own, guarded by a cranky tribe of crows, and the small mountain house in Spain that was our headquarters. Moving was like putting on different lives, different clothes, and we changed easily, falling in with the ways of each country, eating late in Spain, wearing raincoats in Scotland, carrying little from one place to another except the few objects that had become talismans, observing the different domestic rites—of garden and kitchen, mail and garbage.

Since the fifties, I have lived off and on in many different parts of New York, but very intermittently, since I came and went from Spain and from Scotland, never settling decisively in any one of the three. This fall, I returned from a summer spent in Scotland with no apartment—I had given one up before I left, and was expecting another in the spring; but a friend of mine, a dancer, was to be away for a month, and offered me her place in the East Village. I moved in, and took stock.

The apartment itself immediately felt lucky to me, the kind of apartment you want to stay in in, with high windows looking out over St. Mark's churchyard, and light filtered in through leaves to a white, high-ceilinged room, with about a third of the books new to me, and a long Indian file of records. I fell in happily

with the place, explored the neighborhood, and found its Mec-
cas—a Ukrainian butcher shop, pawnshops fat with the appli-
ances of yesteryear, small Indian restaurants that looked as
though they might fold themselves up after dinner and silently
steal away. I made half-hearted attempts to find a more lasting
sublet—buying the *Village Voice* early on Wednesdays, marking
up the *Times* real-estate section on Sunday and then losing it—
but that place made me immune to urgency, although St. Mark's
chimed the hours in my ear.

One evening, I was having dinner with a friend of mine, a
camerawoman, who lives in a loft in SoHo. She moves fast and
often, and always seems to be attached to the ends of five or six
active wires, so when we have dinner, we have a lot of ground to
cover. Over dessert, she suddenly sat up straight. "By the way, I
have to shoot in Arizona most of October. Do you know anyone
who would stay in my loft and look after my cats?" We made a
deal there and then; and, in a flash, I could see the shape of fall
changing. Looking out reflectively on the churchyard the following morning, I realized that I was ideally equipped to be an itinerant. I have an office at the *New Yorker* magazine, where I keep
books and papers, get my mail, and do my writing, when the
time is upon me. What furniture remained to me now graced my
son's apartment, and I was portable, to the tune of two small bags.
I was in touch with other itinerants, some of whom would likely
be going somewhere; and I was myself leaving for South America after Christmas, until the spring. So I dropped the *Voice*, and
went back to reading Michel Tournier's *Friday and Robinson: Life
on Esperanza Island*, my latest bookshelf discovery.

I had never lived in SoHo, and my translation there in October
opened it up to me. I had to have a small course of initiation, in
the hand elevator, in the fistful of keys, in the cats, and then I saw
my friend off in a welter of camera gear—a less portable profession, hers, compared to writing. But then, I have always given
thanks that I did not play the harp. The cats. Alvin, the boss-cat
was called, a massive, broad-shouldered animal who looked as if

he might lift weights in secret. Sadie, his sidekick, was smaller and dumber, but she simpered and purred, which Alvin never did.

Every morning, I fed them first thing, grinding up liver, cleaning their dishes; and when I came back in the evening, they would collar me and drive me toward their empty bowls. The first Saturday, Alvin got through plastic, paper, and close to a pound of sole when I wasn't looking, about an hour after his ample breakfast. But cats are unpunishable by nature, and we came to terms, which meant that I fed them just enough to keep them from breaking into those nerve-rending cries of simulated starvation. Cats in SoHo have the best life going, I concluded, in a loft that must have seemed like an Olympic complex to them, with me to do the shopping. Sometimes I wished they would go out jogging. But I found I could take a brisk walk without leaving the loft, and there was cable television, which kept me up the first couple of nights. Out in the street I learned to stroll all over again, and I connected up SoHo with the rest of Manhattan. I even took to working there, learning how Alvin and Sadie spent their day.

By then, I had come to count on what John Osborne once called "the blessed alchemy of word of mouth," that most human of networks, and it put me in touch with a poet-friend, who was to be away giving readings for a spell in November. Could I stay and look after their plants? Unlike Alvin and Sadie, the plants fed slowly, in a slow seep; and I grew attached to one small fern that required drowning every day, and that rewarded me with new green. Their apartment was in the West Village, the part of New York I have lived in most. The stores were familiar, the kitchen a pleasure to cook in, the books unsurpassable, almost all of them good to read or reread. You can count on poets. Eerily enough, I had stayed in the same apartment once before, on a quick visit from Spain in the sixties, when other friends occupied it. Now it was dressed altogether differently; but every so often, I caught a whiff of its old self and experienced a time-warp, with the kind of involuntary start that often becomes a poem in the end.

As my days there were beginning to be countable, another friend called me, a woman who writes often on Latin America. She was going to Honduras quite soon, and she had two questions: Did I know anyone in Tegucigalpa? Did I know anyone who wanted to rent her apartment for December, while she was gone? Yes to both questions; and, a couple of weeks later, I gave her two addresses in exchange for her keys.

There was, however, a spell in November, between cats, plants, and travels, and also between apartments, when I was saved from the streets by being able to find a room on the Upper East Side. I was finishing a piece on writing at the time, working a long day; but even so I never became a familiar of the Upper East Side, never have. It is hardly itinerants' territory. People don't stroll much there—they seem more purposive, and you have to know where the stores are. You don't stumble on them. It was getting difficult, too, with the subways—I had to think, really *think*, where I was living, Uptown or Downtown, not to go hurtling on the subway in a wrong though familiar direction.

My last resting place lay on the Upper West Side, also a new territory to me, since I have always thought of Forty-fifth Street as the Northern Frontier. It was, however, a revelation. There were oases of movie theaters, comforting even though I never went inside, plenty of odd stores to stumble on, and the neighborhood, to my delight, was Spanish-speaking, even rich in Dominicans, the pleasantest people in Christendom. Moreover, a number of people I had always thought of as out of range turned out to live around the corner. I had had a hasty airport call from my Honduras-bound landlady that morning. "Just pile the papers so you can walk around," she told me tersely. Indeed, her apartment looked as though the negotiations over the Panama Canal had just been hastily concluded in it.

I cleared a camping space first, and then I put the place in order. I have a stern morality about occupying other people's houses: I feel they have to be left in better shape than I find them, and this may mean fixing faucets or supplying anything missing, from light bulbs to balloons. What her apartment needed was restoring to its original order, now only skeletally visible. Anyone who tries to keep up with Central America these days acquires a weekly layer of new information, and her layers went back a few months. When I had the papers rounded up and corralled, the books and records in their shelves and sleeves, the cups and glasses steeping, the place began to emerge and welcome me, and I found, under the sofa, an Anne Tyler novel I had not read. One thing did puzzle me: as I cleaned, I came everywhere on scatters of pennies, on the floor, on chairs, on desk and table, by the bed. I could not account for their ubiquity, but I gathered them in a jar, about enough to buy a good dinner. Christmas was coming to the Upper West Side, with great good cheer; but so was the cold weather, so I went one morning, and booked my air ticket.

Before I left the city, I retraced my wanderings of the fall, going home again and again. If you have lived in somebody's house, after all, you have acquired a lot in common with them, a lot to talk about, from the eccentricities of their pipes to the behavior of their furniture. The tree house by St. Mark's looked properly seasonal, with a fire burning. I find I can still occupy it in my head, with pleasure. I went by the West Village, sat talking for hours in the kitchen, and then walked down to SoHo, where I called on Alvin and Sadie, who looked keenly to see if I had brought fish before withdrawing to rest up. I dropped off a winter coat with my son, and made for the airport and the warm weather with my two bags, leaving behind not one city but several, I felt, shedding a cluster of distinct lives. I just had time to call my friend, newly back from Tegucigalpa. Her time had been good, yes, she had talked at length with my friends, the apartment was great, thanks for fixing the closet door, I had turned up things she thought she'd lost, she felt maybe she had caught a bug in Honduras. I asked her about the pennies. "Oh, yes, thanks for picking them up," she laughed. "It's just that I throw the *I Ching* a lot. Have a good trip."

•

Afterword

Toward the end of 1984, I found land with an enclosed beach on a remote peninsula in the Dominican Republic. I built a small house there, about a mile along the coast from where Columbus made a landfall in January of 1493, and from where he set sail for Spain with the first news of the New World. In his log, he called the landscape "the fairest ever looked on by human eyes" and thought it might indeed be the Garden of Eden.

Printed in the USA
CPSIA information can be obtained
at www.ICGtesting.com
LVHW091515080824
787695LV00001B/115

9 781945 680229